DESIGNER PHOTOSHOP

Designer
PHOTOSHOP

■ ■ ■ ■ ■ ■ ■

by **ROB DAY**

RANDOM HOUSE
ELECTRONIC PUBLISHING

In the memory of
ROBERT FIELDING DAY

Published in the United States by Random House, Inc., New York, and simultaneously in Canada by Random House of Canada, Ltd.

Manufactured in the United States of America.

FIRST EDITION

THIRD PRINTING

Day, Rob.
    Designer Photoshop / by Rob Day.
        p. cm.
    Includes index.
    ISBN 0-679-74394-4
    1. Computer graphics. 2. Adobe Photoshop. I. Title.
T385.D43 1993
006.6'869—dc20   92-21201
                                      CIP

PHOTO CREDITS
Lance Hidy: pages 12-15, 25-30, 32-35, 199, 201, 230, 234
Rob Day: pages 23, 204

New York   Toronto   London   Sydney   Auckland

CONTENTS

ACKNOWLEDGMENTS

I am grateful to the many friends who have helped me with this book. Reading some of the early versions of my text without the benefit of finished illustrations could not have been much fun. Sincere thanks to Claudette Moore, Cindy Ryan, Franklin Davis, Franca Taylor, Rich Day, Steve Dyer, and Mike Prendergast for their valuable suggestions. Also, thanks to Steve Guttman at Adobe Systems for his excellent technical review.

Special thanks to Carl Sesto for teaching me about printing.

Lance Hidy and Etienne Delessert were very generous to take time out from their busy schedules to create beautiful artwork for my book, and I would also like to thank Lance for teaching me how to use Photoshop.

Thanks to all the artists who donated their artwork: Caty Bartholomew, Alan Magee, Barbara Kasten, Sumner Stone, Judy Dater, Javier Romero, Carl Sesto, and Viginia Evans.

And finally, thanks to Virginia Evans for her wonderful design, which I am sure anyone holding this book will appreciate.

INTRODUCTION

This book is for artists, illustrators, and graphic designers who want to use Photoshop as a creative tool. It will also be useful to Photoshop experts who are interested in learning new techniques or seeing how other artists use the program. Because Photoshop is such a complex program, I have not even tried to cover all of its uses; instead, I have demonstrated how I, use the program for real-world and experimental print projects.

In addition to the chapters on creating artwork, there are two chapters on technical issues. The first, *Input,* covers scanning and different types of resolution. Three kinds of resolution interact with one and other in electronic imaging, which can be very confusing to a beginner. Understanding the relationship between pixel resolution and halftone resolution is essential before you start to use Photoshop for print-related projects.

The other technical chapter, *Output,* is important if you expect to use Photoshop for illustration in which color fidelity is important. *Output* covers monitor calibration and how to make the RGB-to-CMYK conversions necessary before going to press. Making a commercially acceptable color separation is the most difficult task that a designer or illustrator faces when using Photoshop. If you create original art with Photoshop, then its color is synthetic—the image as you envision it exists only as it is displayed on your monitor. Professional color separators do not usually rely on monitor displays because their scanners and output devices are under one roof. This means that the scanner can be accurately calibrated to the output device, and the accuracy of the monitor's display is not very important. The separator's only task has been to match output to an *existing* original as accurately as possible.

None of this is possible if you are inventing color and imagery, because your original artwork exists only as it is displayed on your monitor, and chances are your monitor's display looks different than your service bureau's. If you want to take full advantage of the variety of input devices available— from digital cameras to desktop drum scanners—then you must be able to rely on your display. The process of calibrating your monitor to an output device is not difficult, and it is described in detail in Chapter Seven.

When I started writing this book, Adobe was in the process of upgrading Photoshop to version 2.5. All of the figures are captured from screens that appear in the new version, and most of the techniques that I describe are from 2.5 as well. There is also an appendix that describes all of 2.5's new features.

Finally, there are two icons that I have used throughout the text that call out items of special interest. The Note icon indicates text that describes tips and techniques (some of them undocumented) that will make your work more efficient. The Caution icon indicates text that warns you about Photoshop techniques which, if not applied correctly, could cause problems in the creation of an image or in its output. Both of these icons are designed to allow readers quick access to important Photoshop information and make the book easier to use.

R.D.

Auto...

(pixels/inch)

☐ File Size

File
New... ⌘N
Open... ⌘O
Open As...
Place...

1
INPUT

.625   (inches

.435   (inches

Placeme

Acquire ▸ Adobe JPEG Decompress...
          ArrayScan...
          N   3500...

Photograph by Lance Hidy ©1992

■   ■   ■

IN THE SUMMER OF 1989 I had my first chance to try a beta version of Photoshop. The program was very different from the object-oriented drawing programs like Adobe Illustrator that our studio had been using. Photoshop was immediately intuitive—a continuous-tone image could be scanned and instantly twisted, turned, skewed, and electronically painted. After having worked for weeks wrestling with manuals and bezier curves to make the most rudimentary drawings with Illustrator, Photoshop was a liberating experience. The learning curve for creating Photoshop art was not very steep.

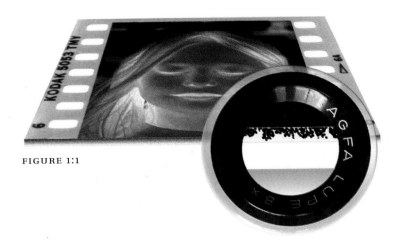

FIGURE 1:1

Photographs are made up of minute silver particles suspended in a gelatin layer on film or paper. The particles are deposited with varying density in the gelatin layer, resulting in the appearance of continuous tone.

My enthusiasm was quickly tempered when I learned how difficult it would be to get the beautiful, glowing images that were displayed on my monitor to the printed page. Again, this was the opposite of Illustrator; as difficult as Illustrator was to draw with, output was relatively simple. At the time there was no hardware or software available for calibrating a monitor, so I never quite trusted the display. It was better to plug in the CMYK percentages that I knew would produce a certain color on press. This was a tedious process, but it generally worked.

Photoshop images are made up of thousands of colored pixels, so plugging in CMYK percentages is not an option. There was also the issue of resolution, which was not a concern with the object-oriented Illustrator. I quickly learned that there is more than one kind of resolution, and that the way color is displayed on a monitor is very different from the the way it prints on paper—my first color separations were murky affairs.

Because of the difficulty of getting what you see on your monitor accurately onto the printed page, I have devoted two chapters to Photoshop production issues. With some careful calibration it is possible to match the final output to your monitor's display, and that will be covered in Chapter Seven. Input, however, is usually the first barrier for new users. This chapter covers scanning techniques, different types of resolution, and how the pixels of an electronic image are translated into the halftone dots of the printed page. I have included as many illustrations as possible to make these concepts clearer. To use Photoshop as a production tool, it is important to have a solid understanding of how images are input.

FIGURE 1:2

Printing presses are not capable of accurately reproducing the varying densities of microscopic silver particles that make up a photograph, so halftone dots are used instead.

HALFTONE DOTS

Most black and white photographs are made up of minute silver particles suspended in a thin layer of gelatin on paper or film. The silver particles are created when light-sensitive silver halide compounds are exposed to light and chemically developed. The amount of light the compounds have been exposed to determines the density of the silver particles on the paper or film. This change in density of silver particles creates different gray values and the appearance of perfect continuous tone in a photograph (**FIGURE 1:1**).

Because printing presses are not capable of reproducing continuous tone images, commercial printers create an illusion of continuous tone with halftone dots. Photographs and artwork are translated into rows of small, varying sized dots by an imagesetter or laser printer (traditional printers use copy cameras and halftone screens). The dots create the appearance of different tones of color when they are printed. If the image is grayscale, 10 percent dots appear as light gray, 50 percent dots appear as middle gray, and so on (**FIGURE 1:2**).

Grayscale images are continuous-tone black-and-white photographs or artwork. True black-and-white images such as wood engravings or pen and ink drawings have no gray values, only black or white.

Printed color images are produced with a composite of four separate halftone screens set at different angles. On press, the four screens are printed using cyan, magenta, yellow, and black ink (CMYK), creating the illusion of a wide spectrum of color. The economy of this system is obvious—running a sheet through the press hundreds of times and printing with different colored inks to reproduce a photograph or artwork would not be commercially viable (**FIGURE 1:3**).

PIXELS

Photographs and artwork are displayed on your monitor in a much different way than halftone pictures on a printed page. A scanner scans and divides a photograph or artwork into a grid of colored squares called *pixels* (an acronym for *picture element*). The more pixels an image is divided into, the higher its resolution. An illusion of continuous tone is created when the pixels become so small that they can no longer be detected. With Photoshop, you can manipulate an electronic picture by changing the hue, value, and saturation of its pixels. Pixels can also be electronically cut and pasted within or between documents (**FIGURE 1:4**).

Four-color printing is a composite of four halftone screens, set at different angles, to create the illusion of many colors.

FIGURE 1:3

*Hue, saturation, and value are words that describe color. Hue is a color's place along the spectrum—red, orange, yellow, green, and so on. Saturation is the brilliance of a color—the more white or black that is added to a hue, the less saturated it becomes. Value is a color's lightness or darkness, independent of hue or saturation (**FIGURE 1:5**).*

GRAYSCALE   Your monitor displays a scan's pixels as different gray values or colors to create the appearance of tonal variation within the picture; the number of values that can be displayed depends on the monitor's *bit depth*. One bit monitors display only two values—black and white. The Macintosh SE and Classic ship with one bit monitors. An 8 bit grayscale monitor can display 256 different values of gray.

Your computer assigns a code of eight 0's and 1's to each value of an 8 bit grayscale. This code is similar to Morse code, in which each letter of the alphabet is assigned a combination of dashes and dots. There are 256 possible combinations of eight 0's and 1's ($2^8=256$), thus the 256 levels of gray (**FIGURE 1:6**). Printing presses are capable of producing only

Computer monitors create an illusion of continuous tone with small, distinctly colored squares called pixels.

FIGURE 1:4

The top row of roses has different hues, the middle row has different saturations, and the bottom row has different values.

Hue

Saturation

Value

approximately 64 distinct grays with one color of ink, so the 256 values that an 8 bit grayscale monitor displays is more than enough information if you are working with grayscale art.

COLOR A monitor capable of 8 bit *color* can display no more than 256 different colors at one time. For accurate display of color images, 256 colors are not enough, so for critical color work 24 bit color is required. A 24 bit monitor can display 256 values for each of its red, green, and blue (RGB) channels,

Each pixel of a grayscale image is described with 8 bits of information. The image's pixels are assigned a code of eight 0's and 1's, which determine its gray level. There are 256 possible combinations of 0's and 1's, to describe 256 different values of gray.

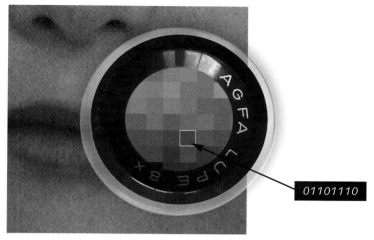

01101110

FIGURE 1:6

increasing the possible number of displayed colors to 16.8 million (2^{24}=16,777,216).

Photoshop has three color modes that are applicable to illustration and design: RGB, CMYK, and Index Color. RGB and CMYK files always contain 24 or 32 bits of information, even if your monitor's display is only 8 bit. Your 8 bit display will not preview Photoshop art as accurately as a 24 bit display, but the output will be the same. If you are using Photoshop 2.5, you can improve the quality of an image displayed on an 8 bit monitor by choosing Use Diffusion Dither from the General Preferences submenu under the File menu. Index Color files are limited to only 256 colors when they are displayed *and* output. An Index Color file size is only one third that of an RGB Color file, but you should not work in this mode if you want high-quality output (**FIGURE 1:7**).

If you are working with an 8 bit display, Index Color is useful for temporarily previewing an image. When you switch to Index Color mode, the preview will appear smoother. After you have previewed the image, return to RGB or CMYK Color by selecting Undo Mode Change (Command+Z) from the Edit Menu.

Monitors and pixels are analogous to a painter's canvas and paint. To reproduce a painting in a book or magazine, usually the artist has the painting photographed and made into a transparency. The transparency is then electronically scanned and output as four color separations, which are used by a printer to make printing plates.

Photoshop art goes through a similar transformation when it is output. A Photoshop image's pixels are translated into halftone dots by an imagesetter, as are the pixels of an electronically scanned transparency (**FIGURE 1:8**). In this case, however, the artist has control over the electronic information and creates the separations as a part of the design process. The imagesetter uses the hue, saturation, and value information contained in the pixels to draw halftone dots at their proper percentages. The step of making a transparency is eliminated because the four-color separations can be generated directly from the information in the electronic file.

BITS AND BYTES

The 0's and 1's that describe the pixel colors of a Photoshop image are called *bits*. The more bits that are needed to describe an image, the more space it will take up in the computer's hard drive or memory. Each image has a file size associated with it measured in kilobytes

24 bit Color

Index Color (8 bit Color)

FIGURE 1:7   *Grayscale (8 bit)*

Black and White (1 bit)

(κ) or megabytes (MB). File size is determined by how many pixels an image is divided into and how many bits are used to describe each pixel (1 bit for black and white, 8 bits for grayscale, and 24 bits for most color). With drawing, page layout, and word processing programs, file sizes are of little concern—most files produced by these programs will easily fit on a floppy disk. Scanned images, however, often create much larger files. File size affects the speed at which your computer can manipulate an image and, in a limited way, the perceived quality of the image when it is output.

You can calculate the amount of space any grayscale scan will take in memory using the following formula:

$$(\text{HEIGHT IN PIXELS} \times \text{WIDTH IN PIXELS}) \div 1,024 = $$
$$\text{FILE SIZE IN KILOBYTES}$$

The pixels of an RGB color image are described with 24 bits (3 bytes) of information, so if the scan is color, multiply the resulting file size by 3. Dividing the file size again by 1,024 gives the size in megabytes. Remember that an image's file size is determined *only* by the number of pixels that it is divided into and the pixels' bit depth, not by the image's height and width. For example, if a scan is 300 x 300 pixels, it can be output as 1"x 1" at 300 pixels per inch, or 10"x 10" at 30 pixels per inch, and the file size will not change (see *Image Size*, **FIGURE 1:9**).

FIGURE 1:9 shows that a scan with only one kilobyte of information does not show much detail when it is output at 2.462"x 2.462". There are only 13 pixels per inch (ppi) in **FIGURE 1:9A**, and the pixels are clearly visible. To make the pixels disappear, the photograph will have to be rescanned at a much higher resolution.

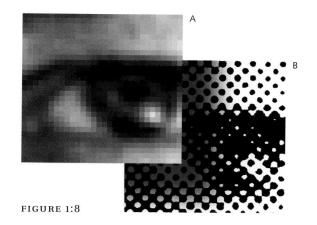

Electronic images are displayed on a monitor as a grid of colored pixels (A). The pixels can be millions of different hues or values, so they must be translated into halftone dots (B) if the image is to be printed economically.

FIGURE 1:8

Image Size

The file sizes of FIGURES A and B are the same, even though their output dimensions are different. This is because both images have the same number of pixels—1,024, making their file size 1,024 bytes or one kilobyte. The width and height at which an image prints out has no influence on its file size.

To manipulate an image's dimensions without changing its file size, open the Image Size dialog box (FIGURE C) under Image in Photoshop's main menu. With the Proportions and File Size boxes checked, Width, Height, and Resolution are constrained. So if Width is changed from 2.462 to 0.5 inches, Height automatically changes in proportion, from 2.462 to 0.5 inches. The resolution also changes proportionally (the size of the pixels becomes smaller) from 13 ppi to 64 ppi (FIGURE D).

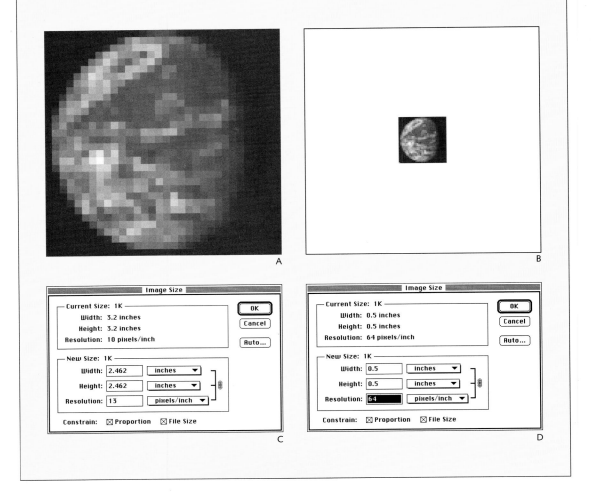

UNDERSTANDING RESOLUTION

For the uninitiated, resolution is certainly one of Photoshop's more difficult concepts. Three different kinds of resolution are associated with electronic publishing, and to add to the confusion all three are often referred to by one term—*dpi*. Pixels per inch (ppi), lines per inch (lpi), and dots per inch (dpi) are distinctly different types of resolution, and to properly input and output images you need to know how they differ.

PIXELS PER INCH A scanner scans and divides artwork or a photograph into a grid of pixels that create an electronic picture (FIGURE 1:4). The pixels of the electronic picture contain the value and color information needed by an output device to translate the image into the halftone dots, which are in turn printed on the page. The more pixels an image is divided into, the higher its resolution; this kind of resolution is called *pixels per inch*, or ppi. If the resolution is high enough, the electronic picture will appear to have continuous tone when viewed on a monitor, and when it is output the pixels will not be visible.

Ppi is often confusingly termed *dpi*. A scanner might be referred to as scanning at 300 dpi, but in fact the scanner divides the picture into 300 pixels, not dots, per inch. The term *dpi* should be reserved for output devices to avoid confusion.

LINES PER INCH Printed images have their own resolution, which is different from the resolution of an electronic image; this resolution is called *lines per inch*, or lpi (FIGURE 1:2). The lpi of a printed image is determined by how many lines of halftone dots the image is divided into. The more lines per inch, the higher the resolution. Lpi varies depending on the quality of the printing job. A newspaper uses approximately 85 lpi, a well-produced magazine may use 133 to 150 lpi, and some art books, where finer detail is desired, might be printed using 200 to 300 lpi.

DOTS PER INCH Dpi is the resolution of an output device. Imagesetters and laser printers output very small dots that make up the letterforms, line art, and halftone dots of a printed page. Each halftone dot is made with the even smaller image-setter or laser printer dots; these dots are sometimes called *spots* or *recorder elements* (**FIGURE 1:10**). Most desktop laser printers print at 300 to 600 dpi, and imagesetters can output at anywhere from 1,200 to 4,000 dpi, depending on the model.

A 300 dpi laser printer's most effective halftone output is at 50 to 60 lpi. If you attempt a higher lpi there will no longer be

Halftone dots are made up of even smaller imagesetter or laser printer dots.

FIGURE 1:10

Each halftone dot is made with smaller imagesetter spots. If you specify a halftone screen that is too high for the output device, the result will be fewer possible gray levels in the printed piece. Figure A was output at 133 lpi from a 300 dpi laser printer. Figure B shows the results when the same file is output at 53 lpi from a 300 dpi laser printer.

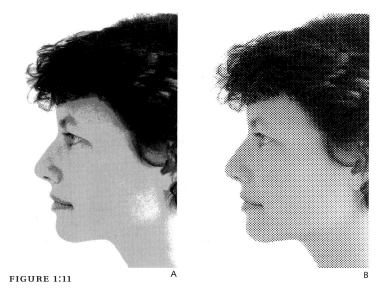

FIGURE 1:11

A

B

enough spots to draw the halftone dot percentages accurately. The resulting printout will start to lose the subtle gradations of a continuous tone-image (**FIGURE 1:11**). Imagesetters must be used when you desire higher halftone frequencies. An imagesetter outputting at 2,540 dpi is capable of accurately producing 150 lpi.

MONITOR RESOLUTION   Monitor resolution adds one final element of confusion to the concept of resolution. A monitor has its own resolution that is independent of image resolution (see **FIGURE 1:12,** *The Monitor's Grid*). Most monitors have a fixed display resolution of 72 pixels per inch, which cannot be changed. With Photoshop you can specify any image resolution. Unless the image resolution is the same as, or a multiple of, the monitor's resolution, the preview displayed on the monitor is either larger or smaller than its output. Not always being able to view a picture at exactly 100 percent takes some getting used to, but the ability to work with any image resolution is worth the inconvenience.

The Monitor's Grid

Photoshop allows you to work at any image resolution. However, your monitor has a fixed resolution that is independent of the image's resolution; most monitors have resolutions of 72 pixels per inch. For display purposes, an image that does not conform to the grid of the monitor is increased or decreased in size.

FIGURE A shows how an image that is 6"x 6" and 100 ppi would look against a 19" monitor's grid. When the image is displayed, it conforms to the 72 ppi of the monitor and appears as 8.33"x 8.33" (FIGURE B). The output dimensions are still 6"x 6" even though the display dimensions are larger.

A

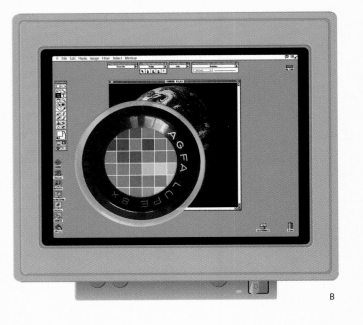

B

IMAGE QUALITY

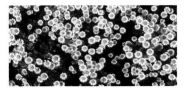

The quality of a printed image can be altered in many ways during the production process whether you work traditionally or electronically. The tendency for many users is to overemphasize the importance of image resolution and ignore other factors that may affect a finished print. Below is a brief description of the production operations that will have an impact on print quality when you work with Photoshop. Most of these operations are covered in greater detail later in the book. Some are more important than others, and depending on time and budget constraints, you may decide to cut corners; if you don't, however, the resulting quality will match most traditional color work.

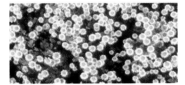

QUALITY OF THE ORIGINAL Photoshop's ability to improve the quality of a mediocre original is remarkable. However, there is a limit to how much can be done to improve a photograph that is out of focus or has poor tonal range. So, unless you are using a bad photograph for artistic effect, pay attention to the quality of the original art.

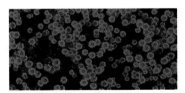

THE SCANNER Scanners differ in capability and price. A $1,200 flatbed scanner will not match the resolution or color fidelity of an $80,000 drum scanner—which is not to say an inexpensive scanner is useless. For the price, a flatbed scanner may be the best piece of hardware you can buy. With some time and skillful color correction, commercially acceptable output is possible with a desktop scanner (see **FIGURE 1:13,** *Comparing Scanners*). The convenience of the flatbed scanner lends itself to the creative process, and if you are heavily manipulating images, a perfect scan may not be necessary. Flatbeds also have the advantage of being able to scan three-dimensional objects. If, on the other hand, you require precise color correction and accurate reproduction of high-quality

Hell DCS-3010   A   Nikon LS-3510AF   B

transparencies, you should purchase scans from trade shops or service bureaus that use high-end scanners.

COLOR CORRECTION   The ability to balance the colors and values of an image is a hard-earned skill. It is also important to be able to calibrate your monitor's display to an output device, so that the output matches what you see on the screen. As soon as you manipulate an image with Photoshop the color of the artwork becomes "synthetic"—the artwork exists only as it is displayed on a monitor. Unfortunately, different monitors often display color differently. This means that your service bureau or trade shop may not have an accurate visual reference to your artwork. Designers have avoided this problem when using page layout or drawing programs by simply inserting CMYK percentages to create a desired color, rather than

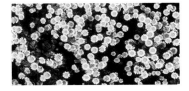

Comparing Scanners

The capabilities of scanners vary depending on the model. FIGURES A, B, and C show the results of the same 35 MM slide scanned on different scanners. FIGURE A was scanned on a Hell DCS-3010, an expensive high-end drum scanner. FIGURE B was scanned on a Nikon LS-3510AF desktop slide scanner ($10,000). FIGURE C was scanned on a Microtek 300Z an inexpensive flatbed scanner ($1,200). Before scanning on the Microtek, I had the slide made into a high quality 4" x 5" Cibachrome print. The high-end scan (FIGURE A) was converted into CMYK by the scanner's software (see *Separation Setup*, Chapter Seven). I color-corrected and used Photoshop's Unsharp Mask filter to sharpen the Nikon and Microtek scans, then converted them to CMYK with Photoshop.

Microtek 300Z　　　　　　　　　C

trusting what they see on their monitors. This strategy is not practical with Photoshop images because they contain thousands of different colors. You must be able to calibrate and rely on your display when using Photoshop (see *Calibration*, Chapter Seven).

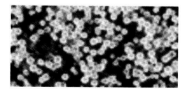

IMAGE RESOLUTION　　The resolution of a scan, measured in pixels per inch, has a profound effect on the quality of output. However, scanning at the highest possible resolution and creating huge files does not necessarily ensure high-quality output. Keep in mind that the ultimate resolution of any printed image is the halftone dot. The pixels of an electronic picture carry the information an imagesetter needs to make the halftone dots. Beyond a certain point—usually between one and two pixels per halftone dot—there is a diminishing return of quality. More than two pixels per halftone dot is wasted information.

Using the correct resolution is important because the image's resolution determines its file size, and file size affects the speed of your computer's operation. Doubling ppi quadruples file size. The larger the file size, the slower your computer will operate, and the longer the imagesetter will take to output the file.

THE HALFTONE SCREEN   It is easy to become too concerned with image resolution and forget about the halftone dot, which is the ultimate resolution of a printed piece. Printers usually use 133 or 150 lpi, and at these screen frequencies it is possible to detect the halftone patterns with the naked eye. Printing presses have limits, so halftone screens are restricted to a relatively low resolution. There are printers who can handle 200- to 300-line halftones, but be prepared to pay a high price for this service. (See **FIGURE 1:14,** *Comparing Halftone Screens*).

CONVERTING RGB TO CMYK   Translating the color electronic image into CMYK halftone separations is both a science and an art. Red, green, and blue (RGB) are the primary colors of your monitor (see Chapter Seven, *Color Models*). This can be confusing for an artist who is used to red, yellow, and blue as the primary colors of his or her paint box.

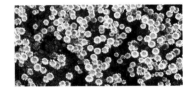

Cyan, magenta, and yellow are the printer's primary colors—cyan and magenta are roughly equivalent to the artist's blue and red, respectively. Using just the CMY separations does produce a large range of color, but unfortunately, in printing, you cannot make black by combining these three colors. When 100 percent CMY are mixed on press the result is dark brown, so a fourth separation must be created for a black plate. There are many options available in Photoshop for making the conversion from RGB to CMYK, that affect the quality of a printed piece (see Chapter Seven for more details on CMYK conversions).

100 lines per inch   **A**

133 lines per inch   **B**

150 lines per inch   **C**

Comparing Halftone Screens

Halftone screen frequency, measured in lines per inch, is the resolution of printed images. The importance of the halftone screen's relationship to image quality is often overlooked. Most commercial printers are limited to 150 lpi.

An effective way to increase the detail in a printed picture is to use a finer halftone screen, but higher screen frequencies require skillful printing. Few commercial printers print with halftone resolutions of more than 200 lpi, and those who can will most likely be more expensive. FIGURES A, B, and C all have the same image resolution—225 ppi—but have different halftone resolutions. FIGURE A is screened at 100 lpi, FIGURE B at 133 lpi, and FIGURE C at 150 lpi.

IMAGESETTERS   Final artwork is output on an imagesetter at a service bureau or color trade shop. Imagesetters output high-resolution film separations, which are used to expose the printing plate. However, imagesetters vary in capability. Make sure that color separations are made by an output device that was designed for multi-color work. The Linotronic 300, for example, is capable of making color separations, but it was designed for one-color work, so the separations may not register well. The Linotronic 330 is a better choice because it was designed for producing accurate color separations.

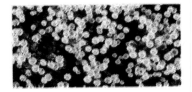

THE PRINTER   Try to work with a printer who is experienced with desktop color separations. If you provide film to a printer who is not familiar with desktop separations and something goes wrong on press, the printer will blame the film, whether or not it is the source of the problem. The ideal printer is one who can make PostScript film in house, or has a close relationship with your trade shop or service bureau.

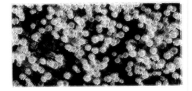

CHOOSING IMAGE RESOLUTION

Before starting work with Photoshop, you must choose an image resolution. This is an important decision because image resolution affects output quality and file size (see **FIGURE 1:15**, *Resolution and File Size*). The more pixels into which an image is divided, the longer it will take a computer to perform operations. File sizes that you can work with are limited by the processing power of your computer and the available disk space. Large files also take an imagesetter longer to output.

The first step in choosing image resolution is to know what the lpi of the printed piece will be. The *Photoshop User Guide* suggests an image resolution of two pixels for every one halftone dot—for instance, if the lpi is 150, then the ppi should be 300. Be aware, however, that two pixels to every one halftone dot is an arbitrary standard based on visual perception rather than any specific need of an output device. If you strictly adhere to this ratio, the file size may become too large for most desktop computers to handle. For instance, a 4"x 5" RGB scan at 300 ppi is 5.15 MB; if you increase the dimensions to 8"x 10", its file size grows to 20.6 MB. With an older computer, you might be able to make some minor color corrections on a twenty-megabyte file, but any complex manipulations will be almost impossible. Adding accelerator boards and large amounts of extra memory helps speed operations significantly, but it is still best to work with the lowest image resolution that produces acceptable detail.

In many cases the 2:1 ratio is too much resolution. You will see very little degradation of image detail when the ratio is lowered to 1.5:1 (see **FIGURE 1:16,** *Comparing Image Resolutions,* and **FIGURE 1:17,** *Changing Image Resolutions*). The 8"x 10" color scan at 225 ppi changes from 20.6 to 11.6 MB. Lowering the ratio to 1:1 causes a slightly more noticeable degradation of image quality, but for many applications this level of quality is

FIGURE 1:15

Resolution and File Size

This graph shows how file size changes as the ppi is increased in an 8"x 10" RGB Color image. Notice that the file size at 150 ppi is about five megabytes. If the resolution is doubled to 300 ppi, the file size quadruples to twenty megabytes.

Unless your computer is fast and equipped with at least 80 MB of memory, it will be almost impossible to seriously manipulate this 20 MB file. By lowering the resolution of the image from 300 to 200 ppi, which would have little effect on its quality (see FIGURE 1:16, *Comparing Image Resolutions*), the file size changes to about 9 MB. Although some operations might still be difficult, this file size is much more manageable.

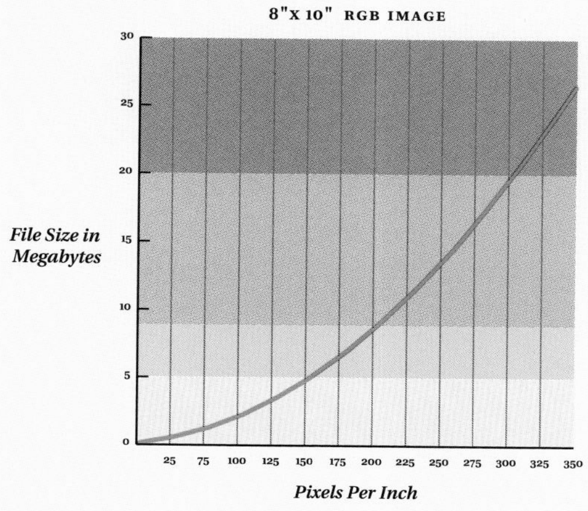

8"x 10" RGB IMAGE

File Size in Megabytes

Pixels Per Inch

300 pixels per inch, 1.46 megabytes   A

225 pixels per inch, 836 kilobytes   B

Comparing Image Resolutions

Above are two different kinds of pictures scanned at various resolutions. The landscape has fine detail and hard edges, while the clouds have mostly soft edges. All of the pictures have a halftone resolution of 150 lpi. The pictures in column A were scanned at 300 ppi. The image resolution in columns B and C was sized down to 225 and 150 ppi, respectively.

The details of the pictures in column C are not as sharply defined as the pictures in the other columns. This degradation in detail is more noticeable in pictures with sharp edges, like the landscape. The change in image detail is subtle, though, and for many applications

150 pixels per inch, 372 kilobytes C

150 pixels per inch with Unsharp Mask applied D

this level of detail is acceptable, particularly if the image is soft-edged, like the clouds.

Any difference in picture detail between columns A and B is barely perceptible, even though the file size of column A's pictures is nearly twice that of column B's. Column D's pictures are 150 ppi with Photoshop's Unsharp

Mask filter applied. The Unsharp Mask Amount was set at 250 percent, the Radius set at 0.5 pixels, and the Threshold set at 1. Skillfully applied unsharp masking can give the illusion of more image detail at lower resolutions.

acceptable. If the image is very detailed with hard edges, such as the texture of rock or the spokes of a bicycle wheel, you may detect a loss in detail, but if the image has soft edges, such as clouds, the change is less noticeable. The 8"x 10" scan at 150 ppi is now 5.15 MB, at 4"x 5" the 150 ppi scan is only 1.29 MB.

 The above discussion of image resolution applies to grayscale and color art only. Black-and-white art—that is, an image in Bitmap mode under Photoshop's Mode menu—must have a much higher resolution to print sharply from an imagesetter. Black and white images should have a resolution of at least 1,000 ppi if they are to be accurately output from a high resolution imagesetter. See Appendix E for a tip on increasing the apparent resolution of a 300-ppi scanner when scanning line art.

SCANNING

Once you have decided on the image resolution and output dimensions of your artwork, its file size in kilobytes (K) or megabytes (MB) can be calculated. For example: the scan is in RGB mode and is to be output at 2"x 2.5" and 150 lpi. Let's also assume that the image is highly detailed so that you will need 1.5 pixels per halftone dot, or 225 ppi. Multiplying both dimensions by 225 gives an image dimension in pixels of 450 x 563. Using the formula given earlier in the *Bits and Bytes* section ([HEIGHT IN PIXELS X WIDTH IN PIXELS] ÷ 1,024 = FILE

Changing Image Resolutions

To change an image's resolution without affecting its width or height, open the Image Size dialog box under the Image menu. Uncheck the File Size box and enter the desired number of pixels per inch in the Resolution box.

FIGURE A was scanned at 400 ppi. FIGURE B has been resampled (pixels added or subtracted) down to 200 ppi. Note that there has been little change in image quality, but the file size has changed significantly—from 2.58 MB to 662 K. Often pictures have too much resolution. If you are making four-color separations, there are not many instances in which 400 ppi are necessary (see FIGURE 1:16, *Comparing Image Resolution*) so you should sample the scan down. The resulting dramatic decrease in file size will be important when you work with artwork that is larger and in color.

FIGURE C has been resampled down even further to 60 ppi, and now there is a very noticeable change in image quality. Resolution can be increased but this practice should be avoided. Photoshop must guess how to add pixels to a picture when you increase resolution, which results in an apparently out-of-focus image. If you need more pixels per inch, rescan at a higher resolution. FIGURE D has been resampled up to 200 ppi from 60 ppi, and the results are not good; if anything, D looks worse than C.

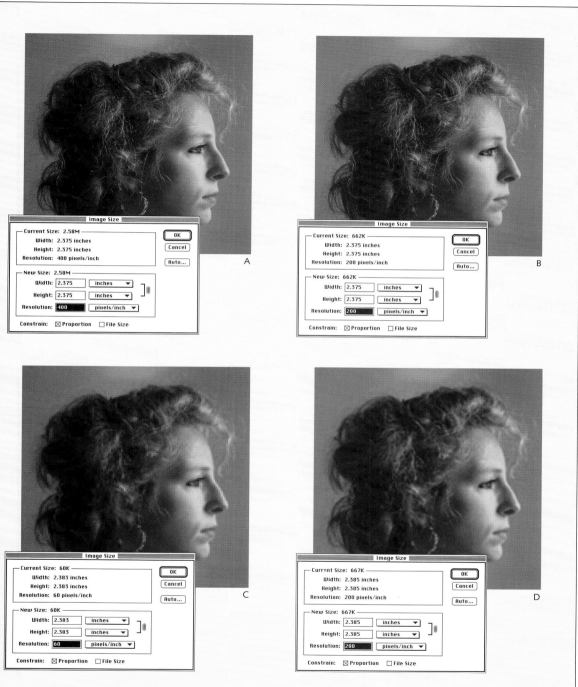

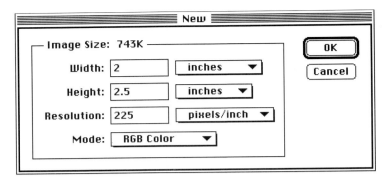

FIGURE 1:18

The New dialog box can be used as a file size calculator. Entering the image dimensions and resolution, and changing the Mode, causes the Image Size to change accordingly.

SIZE IN KILOBYTES), you can calculate the file size to be 743 K.

A faster, easier way to determine file size is to choose New from the File menu. A dialog box appears that you can use as a resolution calculator (**FIGURE 1:18**). Make sure Width and Height are set at inches, Resolution is set at pixels/inch, and, if the scan is color, that RGB Color is checked under Mode. Simply type in the desired width, height, and resolution, and Image Size will change accordingly. Note the file size and click Cancel.

Calculating the file size of a scan in advance can make the scanning process more efficient. The interface for most scanners will provide a preview scan that allows the user to crop and adjust resolution. Usually this preview is not large or clear enough for accurate cropping, and some scanners have a limited number of resolution settings. Interfaces will almost always show the projected file size of a scan, so as long as the scan's file size is adequately large, finished cropping and sizing can be done with more accuracy in Photoshop.

FIGURE 1:19 shows the scanning interface of the Microtek 300z flatbed scanner. This is typical scanner interface, which allows the user to crop and specify dimensions and resolution. Because the preview for cropping is small and at very low resolution, I prefer to make a rough crop in the scanner interface, scan at a higher resolution than necessary, and make the final crop in Photoshop, where it is easier to see the image.

Below is the sequence I use for making an accurate scan:

1. Before scanning, select New from Photoshop's File menu to calculate a target file size. In this case the output dimensions are 2"x 2.5" and the resolution is 225 ppi. Enter 2 and 2.5 in the Width and Height text boxes, respectively, and 225 in the Resolution text box. Make sure the dimensions are set to inches and Resolution is set to pixels/inch. Note the file size—743 K in this case—and click Cancel.

2. After clicking prescan or preview, make a rough crop using the scanner's cropping tool. Change the Resolution and/or Scaling settings until the file size is at least 20 percent larger than the target file size of 743 K (this allows for the further cropping that will be done in Photoshop). This scan should be made at 950 K or higher.

3. Click Scan.

4. After the scan is finished (**FIGURE 1:20**), double-click the Crop tool in Photoshop's tool box, and the Cropping Tool Options dialog box will appear. Make sure that inches are specified. Clicking and dragging on the Size Units text box allows the units to be changed to inches, centimeters,

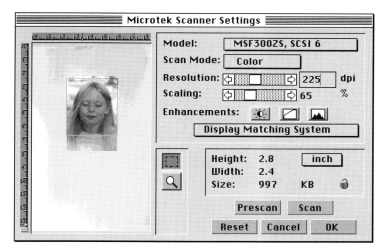

FIGURE 1:19

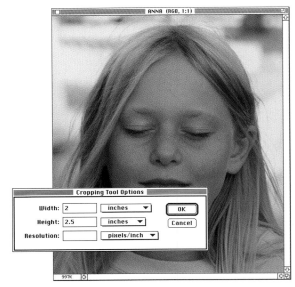

FIGURE 1:20

FIGURE 1:21

points, picas, or columns. Enter the desired width and height, and leave the Resolution box blank. Click OK.

5. Click and drag out the crop marquee. Clicking and dragging on the corner points allows accurate positioning of the marquee (**FIGURE 1:21**), which will be constrained proportionally to the dimensions that were entered into the Cropping Tool Options dialog box.

   Click on the inside of the marquee when you have it in position. The scan will be cropped exactly to the specified dimensions. Resolution is determined automatically by how many pixels are inside of the marquee. The image will not be resampled, so if too much image is cropped, the resolution may end up being less than 225 ppi.

6. Choose Image Size from the Image menu. The dialog box gives the current dimensions (specified earlier in the Cropping Tool Options dialog box) and the image resolution. The current resolution should be higher than the target resolution of 225 lpi.

   Uncheck the File Size box and replace the existing ppi (240 in this case) with 225. If the resolution is significantly lower than 225 ppi, it means the image should be rescanned at a higher resolution. Click OK. The image is resampled and its file size is lowered to 743 K (**FIGURE 1:22**).

Steps 5 and 6 can be skipped by entering the desired resolution along with the width and height in the Cropping Tool Options dialog box (step 4). This will mean that the scan is resized and resampled in one operation. In

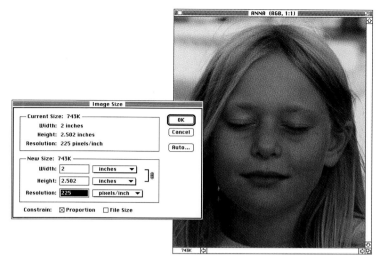

FIGURE 1:22

this case pixels will either be added or subtracted; so be aware that if the initial file size of the scan is not adequately large, the image may be sampled up, which is not desirable (see FIGURE 17D).

Most flatbed scanners have one native scan rate (300 ppi, in the case of the Microtek scanner). If you scan at a percentage of the native scan rate, the resulting scan is interpolated—the scanner skips pixels, making a scan that is not perfectly smooth. I have found that I can get better results by always scanning at the native scan rate, and then resizing the image down in Photoshop. I make sure that the Interpolation method is set at Bicubic in the General Preferences submenu under Edit. This method takes more time but the results are usually of a higher quality.

2
THE PIXEL

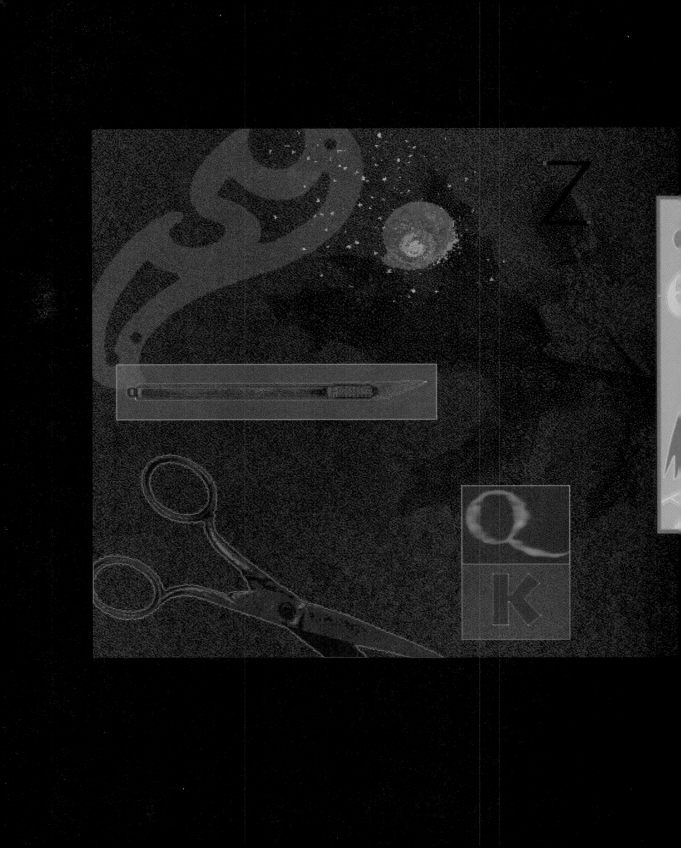

As a printmaker, I learned that every printing method has both advantages and limitations. Silk-screen printing is unequalled in its ability to lay down heavy layers of brilliant, opaque ink, but at the same time it is quite limited if you need high-resolution detail. A woodcut printer often accentuates the wood's texture rather than attempting to hide it—the wood grain becomes part of the design. A good printmaker understands a medium's limitations, and then exploits its strengths.

Pixels are the grain of an electronic image, and they can be used effectively as a design element. The aesthetic of the pixel is a way of avoiding the difficulties associated with large file sizes. Visible pixels means fewer pixels per inch, lower resolution, and smaller file sizes. Sometimes, if your project calls for a large trim size, showing the pixel is the only way to work. Small file sizes also allow for more experimentation—if you want to save an illustration at different stages, multiple copies of ten- to twenty-megabyte files will put a strain on your storage space.

In January 1990 I received an assignment to illustrate the software package for a program called Interleaf Publisher 1.1. Our studio had been using a beta copy of Photoshop for about six months, and we had had some success making four-color separations from Photoshop, so this seemed like an ideal project for combining Adobe Photoshop and Illustrator. I have chosen to demonstrate this project because it covers some of Photoshop's most basic tools, and its file size (984 K) was very small relative to its trim size, which makes it accessible to users with slower machines.

At the time, my hardware was a Macintosh II with 5 MB of RAM and a 40 MB hard disk. The illustration's trim size was 17" x 9.75". If I had tried to work with fully resolved images, the file size would have been nearly 24 MB. This was out of the question on a slow computer with such a small amount of disk space. I also had a deadline of less than two weeks, so I could not afford to struggle with a large file size.

Photoshop requires a combination of available memory and open disk space that is three to five times larger than the file size being worked on. For more information on how Photoshop uses disk space, see Appendix D, Faster Photoshop.

By using the pixel as a design element, I could reduce the file size to less than a megabyte. The small file size allowed me to experiment and save the illustration at different stages without filling my limited storage space. This flexibility is very important for users who have older, slower machines, and for beginners who are learning the program. Since the illustration was originally made using Photoshop 1.0, I have recreated it here taking advantage of 2.5's features.

Interleaf Publisher is a software package designed for publishing long and complex documents. The program integrates page layout, drawing, and spreadsheet features into one piece of software. The concept for the illustration was to combine with natural objects the traditional tools that the software emulated, giving a feeling of elegance. The illustration wraps around the software box, which has a six-inch spine. A hard-edged drawing of tools and letterforms created with Adobe Illustrator floats on the spine.

SCANNING AND CROPPING

I started the illustration with a black-and-white photograph of a leaf half buried in sand, which I had shot at a local beach. You can use any grayscale scan if you would like to follow this exercise. The negative was scanned with a Nikon LS-3500 slide scanner. I wanted to create a fairly coarse texture, so before making the scan, I experimented with different resolutions to determine how large the pixels should be, and settled on 45 ppi. I calculated the finished grayscale scan's size would be 328K (see Chapter One, *Accurate Scanning*), and then made the scan at about 500 K so that there would be plenty of room for cropping.

After scanning, I named and saved the untitled file by choosing Save (Command+S) from the File menu. The Save dialog box has a pop-up menu for choosing a file format; the default for new documents is Photoshop. I recommend using the Photoshop format when you are working on an illustration. Other file formats are covered in Appendix A, *File Formats*.

Next, I double-clicked on the Crop tool and entered the dimensions (17" x 9.75") and resolution (45 ppi) in the Cropping Tool Options dialog box (**FIGURE 2:1**). I then pulled out the marquee until it surrounded the part of the image that I wanted to crop. When you move the cursor inside of the marquee, it becomes a scissor icon; clicking makes the crop (**FIGURE 2:2**). Because I had entered the crop's resolution and dimensions in the Cropping Tool Options dialog box, the leaf scan was resized and resampled in one operation after I clicked inside of the marquee.

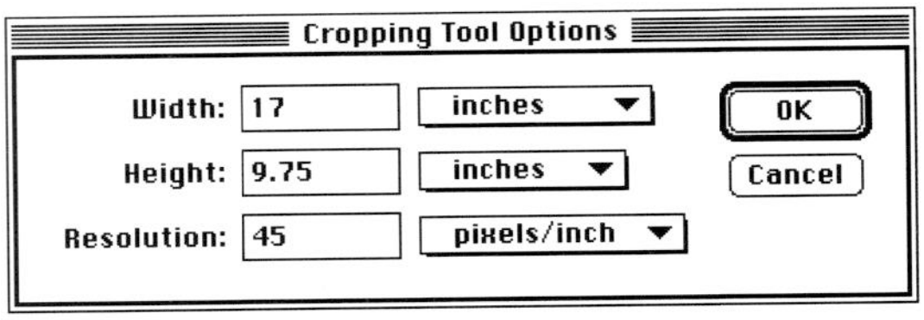

> *If you hold down the Option key and click and drag on a crop marquee's corner points, the marquee can be rotated. You can also move the marquee without changing its size by holding down the Command key, then clicking and dragging on a corner point.*

FIGURE 2:1

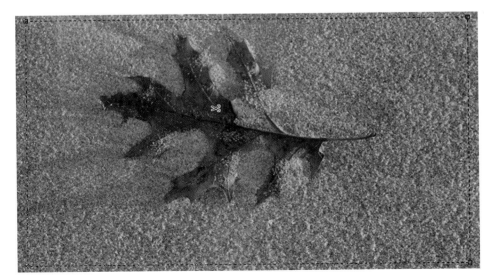

FIGURE 2:2

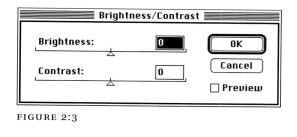

FIGURE 2:3

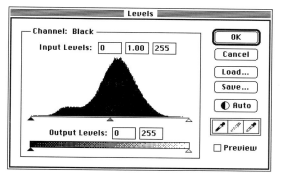

FIGURE 2:4

ADJUSTING A GRAYSCALE

After making the crop, I adjusted the brightness and contrast of the leaf scan. Photoshop has a number of tools designed for adjusting a picture's grayscale; the differences among them are in ease of use and sophistication. You will find that taking the time to master Photoshop's color correction tools is worth the effort. Below is an overview of three dialog boxes for adjusting an image's values. All three are found in the Adjust submenu, under the Image menu.

BRIGHTNESS / CONTRAST   The easiest, but least sophisticated, way to adjust value is with Brightness/Contrast. The dialog box is self-explanatory—moving the top slider right or left lightens or darkens the image. Moving the bottom slider increases or decreases contrast (**FIGURE 2:3**).

LEVELS   Levels is less straightforward, but has more options than Brightness/Contrast. The Levels dialog box shows a graph labeled

Input Levels with three small adjustment triangles beneath its baseline, and below that a grayscale bar labeled Output Levels with two small adjustment triangles (**FIGURE 2:4**).

The Input Levels graph (also called a histogram) is a representation of the 256 possible gray levels in the currently selected area (or in the entire picture, if nothing is selected), from 0 on the left representing pure black, to 255 on the right representing pure white. Each vertical black line represents the number of pixels in the image or selection at a given level along the grayscale. Images with good contrast will show a Levels graph with vertical lines that are spread across the entire scale from white to black. Conversely, an image with low contrast will show a graph with the vertical lines clumped in one spot. FIGURE 2:4 shows the Levels dialog box for the finished scan of the leaf. The graph shows that the values in the leaf cover almost the entire grayscale, resulting in an image with good contrast. Most of the pixels in the image are middle grays; this is indicated by the large mound of vertical lines in the middle of the graph.

If you click and drag on any of the small triangles in the Levels dialog box, the grayscale of the image changes interactively. When you click OK, the changes are applied to the currently selected area or, if nothing is selected, to the entire image. The middle triangle beneath the Input Levels graph adjusts the mid-tones of an image without significantly affecting the highlights or shadows. Photographers refer to this mid-tone change as *gamma adjustment*. Sliding the middle triangle to the left lightens the image; sliding it to the right darkens the image. Sliding the white triangle on the right to the left brightens the highlights; moving the black triangle on the left to the right darkens the shadows. Both of these moves increase the contrast of the image.

If you adjust the two triangles under the Output Levels grayscale bar, the image loses contrast. Moving the white triangle on the right darkens the highlights, and moving the black triangle on the left lightens the shadows. The ability to adjust these five triangles gives you much more control over the image's values than you have using the Brightness/Contrast tool.

One of Photoshop 2.5's new features is a powerful Preview option included in all of the color-correcting dialog boxes. The Preview option is now a check box rather than a radio button. If the Preview box is checked, the changes you make do not happen interactively to the entire screen. However, each time you release the mouse button, the current selection is updated with the new change. The nonselected portions of the image remain unchanged. If the Preview box is left unchecked, then the changes occur interactively, but to the entire screen, as was the case with 2.0. In this case, to see the changes only in the selected areas, you must click OK.

CURVES   Curves gives you the most control adjusting an image's values. Traditional electronic pre-press systems have controls for adjusting color and value that the Curves dialog

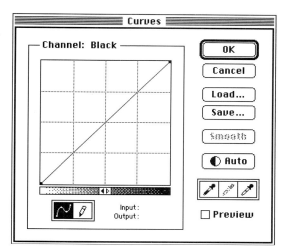

FIGURE 2:5

box is modeled after. The Curves dialog box shows a graph that plots the Input levels (the values, from 0% to 100%, in the picture as they currently exist) on the horizontal x axis against the Output levels (the new values as you adjust the curve) on the vertical y axis (**FIGURE 2:5**).

When you open the Curves dialog box, the line on the graph is diagonal because the Input and Output values are the same. Clicking on the diagonal line plots a point that can be adjusted. For instance, if you click on the center of the diagonal line, Input and Output both read 50%. By pulling the point straight down, the Output readout changes to a smaller percentage while Input remains the same. This means that the 50% middle gray will be lightened to the new Output percentage. The image's other values will also be lightened, but on a gradual curve until there is no change at the 0 and 100% levels (**FIGURE 2:6**). This curve increases contrast as the image is lightened or darkened.

Plotting multiple points along the curve allows control over different portions of the image's grayscale. For example, if you want to affect only an image's quarter-tones, plot a point on the diagonal's center mark so that the readout is Input: 50% and Output: 50%, then plot another point at Input: 25% and move the 25% point up or down. This will darken or lighten the quarter-tones, while the mid-tones stay anchored.

Notice that when the cursor is outside of the dialog box and on the active window it becomes an eyedropper. Clicking on the image with the eyedropper creates a circle on the curve that relates to the pixel that has been clicked on. If you want to lighten or darken a specific gray level of an image, click on it with the eyedropper and note where the circle appears on the curve. Then plot a point there and move it up to darken, or down to lighten that part of the grayscale (FIGURE 2:7). If you are working in CMYK mode, the eyedropper works only when the C, M, Y, or K radio button is clicked on.

> *You can adjust the way the Eyedropper cursor reads the pixel information by double-clicking on the Eyedropper tool and choosing either Point Sample, 3 by 3 Average, or 5 by 5 Average. Choosing 3 by 3 or 5 by 5 Average prevents you from choosing a random pixel value that is not representative of the values in the area you click on.*

There is a grayscale bar at the bottom of the Curves dialog box, showing the progression of gray values on the x axis, from white (0%) on the left to black (100%) on the right. If you click on the grayscale bar it is reversed, to black on the left and white on the right. Also, instead of the readout appearing as a percentage, it appears as a grayscale level from 0 to 255.

CREATING A BITMAP

After adjusting the gray values of the leaf scan, I converted it to a dithered bitmap by selecting Bitmap under Mode. You must be in grayscale mode in order to select Bitmap. Dithered bitmaps are made of only black and white pixels, and have a mezzotint-like texture. Tonal variation is created by spacing the black or white pixels at different intervals, rather than by

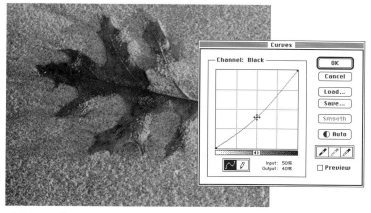

FIGURE 2:6

FIGURE 2:7

Moving the cursor outside the Curves dialog box changes it to an Eyedropper cursor. Clicking causes a circle to appear on the curve that corresponds to the value of the pixel under the tip of the eyedropper.

This tool is useful for choosing specific gray levels of the image that you want to adjust. In this case, the gray level I will adjust is 27%.

By plotting a point at the 50% and 75% marks of the graph, I have anchored the mid- and three-quarter tones, allowing me to brighten the quarter tones independent from the other tones. Here I have changed the 27% values to 18%. The Curves Eyedropper cursor works only with grayscale images or the individual channels of a color image.

increasing or decreasing their size. When you choose Bitmap from the Mode menu, a dialog box appears giving you a choice of different bitmap patterns (**FIGURE 2:8**). The Bitmap option converts the image's 256 level grayscale into two levels—black and white. When you choose Diffusion Dither and click OK, a dialog box appears allowing you to change resolution (the size of the pixels). In this case I wanted the resolution to remain 45 ppi, so I clicked OK (**FIGURE 2:9**).

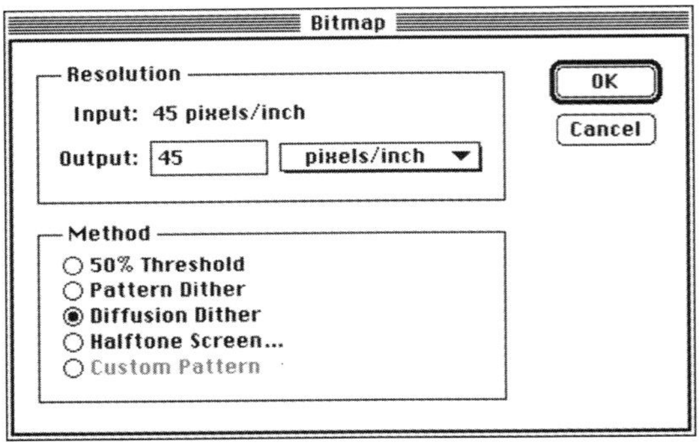

FIGURE 2:8

FIGURE 2:9

Once I had converted the leaf grayscale into a bitmap, I changed the mode of the image back to Grayscale and then to RGB Color. The image still appears to be black and white, but it can now be colored. Its file size has grown from 42 K to 984 K, a factor of 24 that reflects the change from 1 bit to 24 bit.

 Every Photoshop file shows its current file size in its window's lower-left corner. If you hold down the Option key and click on the left corner, a pop-up box will appear showing information about the file—the width and height in both pixels and inches, the number of channels, the mode, and the image resolution.

MAKING SELECTIONS

I wanted to change the color of the white pixels, but I had to select them first. Photoshop has five tools designed for selecting parts of an image. Once part of an image is selected, it can be worked on independently. A selected area is indicated by a dotted line moving around its edges. Below is a quick overview of Photoshop's selection tools:

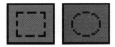 **RECTANGULAR AND ELLIPTICAL**   The top two icons in the tool box represent the most basic selection tools, the Rectangular and Elliptical marquees. They allow you to quickly click and drag out rectangular, square, circular, and elliptical selections. Double-clicking on either icon brings up a dialog box that allows you to specify exact pixel dimensions or aspect ratios for a selection. If you are using Photoshop 2.5, you can now apply a feather to rectangular and elliptical selections in these dialog boxes. For more on feathering, see Chapter Five.

 LASSO   The Lasso tool is used for making manual, irregular selections. You draw the selection freehand, which can be difficult with a mouse, so it takes some practice. By clicking and dragging, you can create a selection line around any area of the image. When you release the mouse button, the two ends of the lasso line are automatically connected. This can be frustrating if you accidentally release the mouse button. However, with the Option key pressed, you can release the mouse button without the selection being automatically completed. Also, if you move the mouse with the button released and the Option key pressed, a straight line is pulled out that can be anchored with a click of the mouse button. This is an effective way to select hard-edged shapes.

MAGIC WAND   The Magic Wand is used for automatically selecting areas of an image that have similar value and color. Double-clicking on the icon opens a dialog box that allows you to set a tolerance. If you increase the tolerance number, then more values will be added to the selection; the default is 32 with Anti-aliased checked. Checking Anti-aliased makes the edge of the selection smoother.

Sometimes after drawing a selection, you may want to add areas to or subtract them from a selection. If you want to add to a current selection using any of the above tools, hold down the Shift key and make an additional selection. The new selection will be added to the existing selection. If you want to subtract from a selection, hold down the Command key; whatever you draw that intersects with an existing selection will be removed from the selection. You can also easily adjust a selection by using Photoshop 2.5's new Quick Mask feature, which is covered in Chapter Four.

PEN   The Pen tool allows you to draw very accurate selections made with straight lines and curves, called bezier curves, that have anchor and control points. You can then select the anchor and control points and manipulate them at anytime. If you are familiar with drawing programs such as Adobe Illustrator and Aldus Freehand, this tool will be easy to use. If you are still using version 2.0, you click on the Pen icon in the tool box, then click on the image. Clicking on the image launches a mini-program within Photoshop, and new menus will appear. Clicking and dragging lays down anchor and control points that allow you to create smooth curves. When a path is completed, you can save it and then load it at any time from the Selection menu using the Load Path command. This is helpful if you have spent some time creating a path and want to access it later. Clicking inside of a path transforms it into a selection and restores the Photoshop menu bar.

2.5'S PEN TOOL   The Pen tool has been made more powerful in Photoshop 2.5. It has been moved from the tool box to a floating palette, called Paths, accessed from the Window menu (**FIGURE 2:10**). Show Paths shows the palette, Hide Paths hides the palette. This new palette makes the Pen tool easier to use. When you click on the Pen icon in the palette's window, you do not launch a mini-program, as is the case if you are using Photoshop 2.0. Now when you draw with the Pen tool you can interrupt the drawing process and access any of Photoshop's menus and tools. The new Pen tool is closer to Adobe Illustrator in its function. If you are not used to drawing with bezier curves, read the section on the Pen tool in the *Adobe Photoshop User Guide*.

SELECTING THE WHITE PIXELS

To select the leaf's white pixels, I first zoomed in until the pixels were clearly visible. Holding down the Command key and Spacebar temporarily accesses the Magnifier tool when any other tool is active; clicking on the image magnifies the preview, doubling its size with every click. Only the preview changes size; the window size remains the same. Adding the Option key to Command and Spacebar allows you to zoom back out. Another

The Paths Palette

The Pen tool has been moved to a floating palette called Paths in Photoshop 2.5. Clicking on the arrow in the upper-right corner accesses a pop-up menu that allows you to manage paths:

• By Choosing Save Path you can save and name paths that you create. Each saved path appears in a list in the palette. You can load a saved path by clicking on its name. A loaded path has a check mark to the left of its name.

• You can delete a path by choosing Delete Path when the Path's name is checked.

• You can convert any path that you create or load, into a selection by choosing Make Selection.

• You can transform a selection, created with any of the selection tools, into a path by choosing Make Path.

• You can fill and stroke paths. When you choose Stroke Path, you can select any of the painting tools from a pop-up menu (FIGURE B), then stroke a loaded path with the current foreground color using the brush that is active in the Brushes palette.

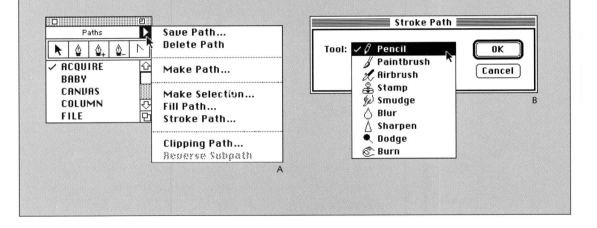

A

B

way of zooming in on an image is Command++. To zoom out, use Command + -. In this case, the window size increases or decreases along with the preview.

If you want to quickly zoom in on a specific part of an image, click and drag when the Magnifier tool is selected (Command + Spacebar), and a marquee will appear. Drag the marquee to surround the part of the image on which you want to zoom in. When you release the mouse button, the image area inside of the marquee will fill the window (in version 2.0, the image fills the screen). Double-clicking on the Magnifier icon in the tool box returns the preview to a 1:1 ratio.

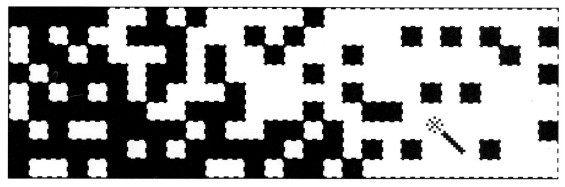

FIGURE 2:11

I magnified the leaf image until the pixels were large enough to easily select an area of pixels with the Magic Wand. In this case, I wanted to select only one pixel color—white—so I entered a Tolerance of 0 and left Anti-aliased unchecked. Clicking once selects the pixel clicked on and any adjoining pixels of the same color, white in this case. I wanted to make sure *all* of the white pixels were selected, so I chose Similar from the Select menu; this selects all of the pixels in the image that are similar to the current selection. In this case all of the white pixels were selected (**FIGURE 2:11**).

 *There is an even faster way to select all of the white pixels in a dithered bitmapped image that has been converted to RGB Color. Choose Duplicate from the Calculate submenu under the Image menu. Keep the Source as your bitmapped image, choose Red (Green or Blue would also work in this case) from the Source Channel pop-up menu, and choose Selection from the Destination Channel pop-up menu. Click OK and the white pixels will be selected (**FIGURE 2:12**).*

COLORING THE BITMAP

With all of the white pixels selected I could now color them. At the bottom of Photoshop's tool box is a black box overlapping a white box. The foreground black box is used for choosing a foreground color; the background white box is for selecting a background color. I clicked on the black box. This opens Photoshop's Color Picker (see **FIGURE 2:13,** *Choosing Color*).

I wanted to change the white pixels of the leaf bitmap to teal green, so I chose the green I wanted and clicked OK. The teal green now appears in the foreground color box in place of the black. I filled the selected white pixels with the green by holding down the Option key and pressing Delete (**FIGURE 2:14**). This is a shortcut to choosing Fill from the Edit menu. Pressing only the Delete key fills a selected area with the current background color.

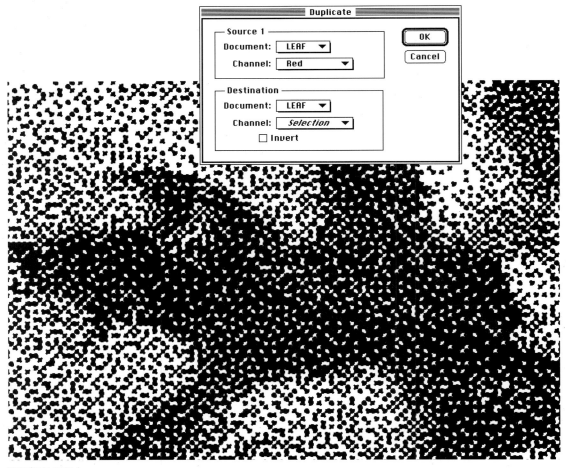

FIGURE 2:12

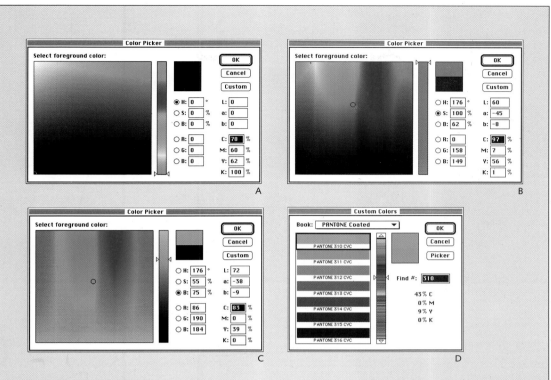

Choosing Color

Photoshop provides a number of options for choosing color. Open the Color Picker by clicking on either the black or white square at the bottom of the tool box menu. The black square is for the foreground color and the white square is for the background color. FIGURE A shows the default color picker.

The largest square shows hue with white added on the horizontal axis and black added on the vertical axis. You can change hue by moving the triangle to the right of the box up or down along the rainbow colored bar. The colored boxes to the right of the hue slider show the existing color on the bottom and the new color at the top. Clicking and dragging inside of the large box changes the new color to correspond to the color beneath the cursor— or you can enter any desired CMYK percentage in the boxes at the far right. Clicking on the S, B, R, G, or B radio buttons gives variations on the default color picker. FIGURES B and C show the S and B pickers.

Once you have chosen a color, you can click on Custom to access a variety of custom color systems such as Pantone or Trumatch (FIGURE D). The color that you chose in the Color Picker is the color selected in the custom system or its closest match. Also, if you choose a new color from the custom color selector and then click on Picker, you return to the Photoshop Color Picker and the custom color that you chose will be selected.

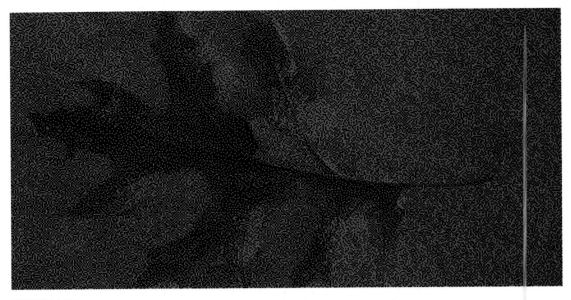

FIGURE 2:14

Next I wanted to change the color of the black pixels. I chose Inverse from the Select menu. This reversed the selection so that all of the black pixels were selected. I changed the foreground color from teal to a reddish brown, and again pressed Option+Delete to change the black pixels to brown (**FIGURE 2:15**).

 The currently selected part of an image is surrounded by a moving marquee, which can be distracting, particularly with complex selections. Choose Hide Edges (Command+H) from the Select menu to temporarily hide the selection marquee—but be careful you don't forget that there is a hidden selection. If one of the painting tools will not work correctly, chances are it is because there is a hidden selection—the painting tools will not work on any part of the image outside of a selection. Choose Show Edges (Command+H) to make the selection marquee show again.

COLOR CORRECTING

With the black and white pixels changed to colors, I could now fine-tune the two colors in a number of ways. I could simply choose new colors with the color picker and then fill them—inverting the selection to switch between the two colors—or I could use the color-correcting tools to adjust the color interactively. In this case, the green I had chosen needed to be slightly bluer, so I inverted the selection to select the green pixels. Choosing Color Balance from the Adjust submenu under the Image menu (Command+Y) opens the Color Balance dialog box, which allows you to adjust the current selection's color balance. The dialog box shows three horizontal lines with cyan, magenta, and yellow on the left, and red, green, and blue on the right; moving the center triangles adjusts the color of the current selection. You can also choose to affect the shadows, midtones, or highlights by clicking the radio buttons at the bottom of the dialog box. In this case, to make the green bluer, I selected Midtones, slid the bottom triangle to the right toward blue and the top triangle to the left toward cyan, and clicked OK (**FIGURE 2:16**).

At this stage, the bitmap had a very uniform texture, so I decided to add some noise (noise adds a grainy texture to an image). First I chose All from the Select menu (Command+A) to select the entire image, then I chose Add Noise from the Noise submenu under the Filter menu. A dialog box appears that allows you to assign a numerical value to specify how heavy the noise will be. I entered 20 in the Amount box and clicked OK (**FIGURE 2:17**). Increasing the amount increases the coarseness of the grain.

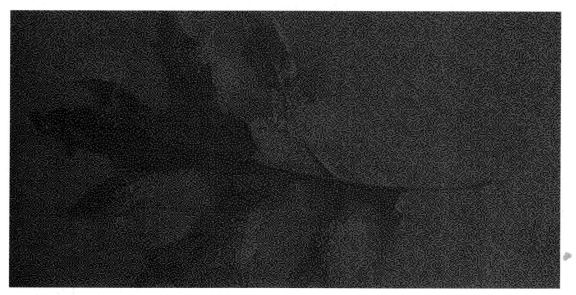

FIGURE 2:15

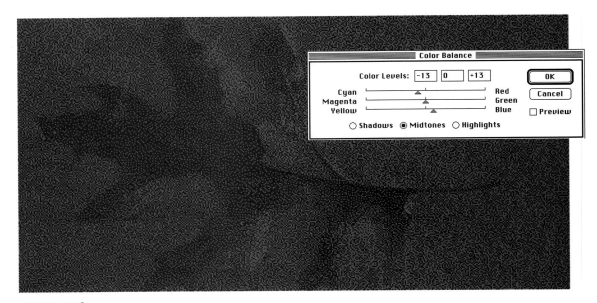

FIGURE 2:16

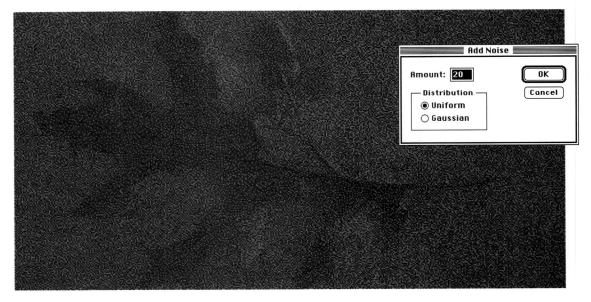

FIGURE 2:17

FIGURE 2:18

SAVING

After coloring the leaf, the next step was to start cutting and pasting the tools and natural objects. Once you have pasted an object, it cannot be easily moved. If you reselect and then attempt to move a pasted object, a hole will be left in the shape of the selection. The hole will be filled with the current background color. If you are using Photoshop 2.5, there is a new feature under the Select menu called Float (Command+J). This creates a floating copy of the selection so that when you move the selection there will not be a hole. I decided to save a copy of the colored leaf in case I needed to revert to it later. As is the case with any computer program, saving often is important, and if you can afford the disk space, saving copies of an illustration at different stages is worthwhile.

To make a copy of a file, first save it (Command+S).This is very important. Next, choose Save As from the File menu and type a new name into the Save this Document as Text box. Keep the File Format as Photoshop 2.0 or Photoshop 2.5, and click OK. Notice that the name in the title bar changes to the new file name. I continued to work on the new file. The older version of the file was the colored leaf as it was last saved. This is the way most programs handle Save As. If you are using version 2.5, Save As will work this way no matter which format you choose. However, if you are working with Photoshop 2.0 and you chose any file format other than Photoshop, the newly named file is saved to disk as it currently exists, and you continue to work on the old file. Notice that the title bar does not change in this case. This dual nature of Save As in version 2.0 is very confusing, so be careful.

CUTTING AND PASTING

With the leaf colored, I now started adding the other elements of the collage. I scanned the tools on a Microtek 300z flatbed scanner; the natural objects were from black-and-white photographs taken at the beach and scanned on the Nikon slide scanner (**FIGURE 2:18**). Before making the scans, I estimated how large the objects would be on the finished piece and calculated the file size based on 45 ppi. I made sure the scans were slightly larger than they needed to be, so that when I scaled them to the desired size I would always be scaling down. Scaling works the same way as resizing—it is always best to reduce the size of an image so that Photoshop is removing, rather than adding, pixels to the image.

You cannot have different resolutions in the same Photoshop file. When you attempt to paste an image that is 2"x 2" and 90 ppi onto a 45 ppi image, the pasted object's dimensions will double in size when it is pasted, because it must conform to the grid of the 45 ppi image. If you are having trouble with pasted objects being too large and overflowing the window they are pasted into, see **FIGURE 2:19**, Pasting and Resolution.

After making the scans, I selected the objects so I could cut them from their backgrounds and paste them onto the leaf bitmap. I used the Magic Wand to select the sand dollar and shell, and the Pen tool to select the other objects. For the shell, I double-clicked on the Magic Wand, entered a Tolerance of 20, then clicked OK. I then clicked once on the sand behind the shell; this selected everything except the shell and the darkest grains of sand, which in the final illustration have a celestial

Pasting and Resolution

FIGURE A shows what can happen if you attempt to paste a high-resolution image into a low-resolution window. To ensure that a cut or pasted object pastes at the proper size into another window:

1. Preview the window that you want to paste into alongside the window with the selection that you are cutting or copying from.
2. Typing Command + + or Command + – increases or decreases the preview size of the active window; the ratio in the title bar changes accordingly. Adjust one or both windows until the title bar ratios are the same (FIGURE B).
3. If the selection that you plan to copy appears to be larger than the window it is being pasted into, you should resize it. Click on its title bar and choose Image Size from the Image menu. With Proportions checked and File Size unchecked, enter a lower resolution or dimension. Click OK and the window size will become smaller while its ratio stays the same (FIGURE C). When you resize the image, any current selection will be lost, so resize before you make the selection.
4. You can now make a selection, copy it, and it will paste inside of the destination window's border (FIGURE D). Choosing Scale from the Effects submenu under the Image menu allows you to reduce the pasted object's size further if necessary.

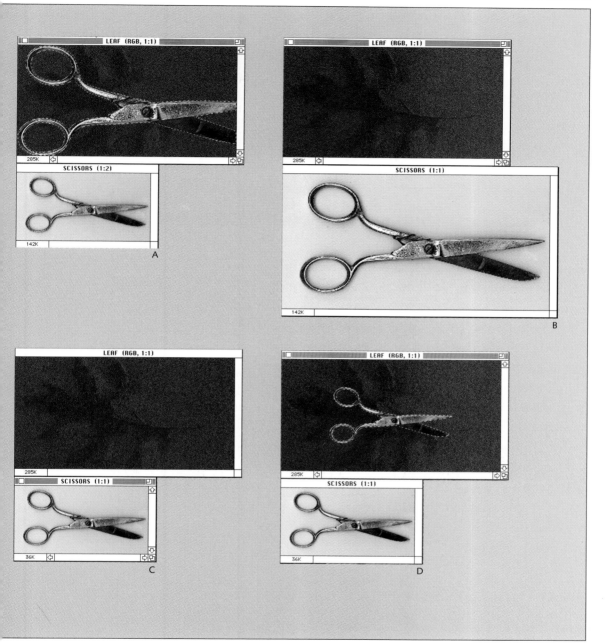

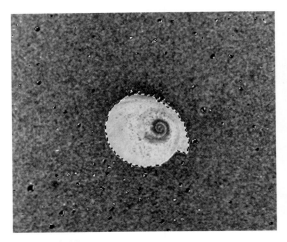

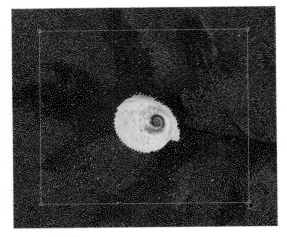

FIGURE 2:20   FIGURE 2:21

appearance. I inverted the selection by choosing Inverse from the Selection menu to select the shell and the grains of sand (**FIGURE 2:20**). I then copied the selection (Command+C), clicked on the leaf's window, and pasted the shell (Command+V). The shell is now a floating selection that can be easily moved and resized until it is deselected.

To move a selection, one of the selection tools (the Rectangular, Elliptical, Lasso, or Magic Wand tool) or the Type tool must be highlighted in the tool box. When you move the cursor inside of the selection, it turns into a right-pointing arrow. Clicking and dragging moves the selection. Be careful not to click outside of the selection or it will be deselected. If any of the other tools are selected, you can move a selection by holding down the Command key and then clicking and dragging inside of the selection.

SCALING AND ROTATING

The floating shell was too large, so I resized it by choosing Scale from the Effects submenu under Image. The shell was now surrounded by a marquee with adjustment points in the corners. Clicking and dragging on the corner points allowed me to resize

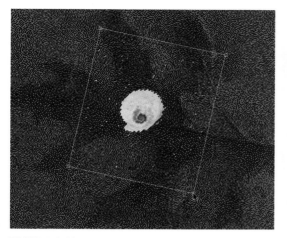
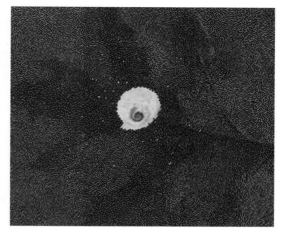

FIGURE 2:22

the selection. If you hold down the Shift key while dragging, the resizing is constrained proportionally—the image will not be distorted (**FIGURE 2:21**). After I resized the shell, I wanted to rotate it, so I chose Free from the Rotate submenu under Image. Again, a marquee with corner points appeared that I clicked on and dragged to rotate the selection (**FIGURE 2:22**).

 The Rotation, Distortion, and Scaling tools have been changed with Photoshop 2.5. Now when you scale or rotate a selection, you are adjusting a preview—this lets you quickly see different choices. The Preview feature allows you to size the selection down and then up again without effectively lowering its resolution. Once you have settled on an adjustment, you must click inside of the marquee to have the change take effect.

I wanted to color the objects before they were permanently pasted onto the leaf, so I created a new document for each of the resized parts. When I finished rotating and resizing the shell, I cut it (Command+X), then chose New (Command+N) from the File menu. This displayed a dialog box containing options for specifying the dimensions and mode of the new

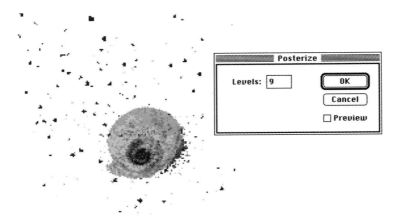

FIGURE 2:23

document. The default setting reflects the dimensions and color mode of what is currently on Photoshop's clipboard—in this case the shell. I made no changes and clicked OK. A new window appeared filled with the current background color. I pasted the shell into this new window.

COLORING THE PIECES

Next, I posterized the resized shell. I chose Posterize from the Map submenu in the Image menu (posterizing an image limits its gray levels to a specified number). A dialog box appeared that allowed me to specify the number of gray levels in the current selection. I entered 9 and clicked OK (FIGURE 2:23). The shell's grayscale was converted from 256 to 9 levels of gray. Each gray value could now be quickly selected with the Magic Wand and colored. Before coloring the posterized shell, I made a negative of it by choosing Invert from the Map submenu. It was the only object that I made negative (FIGURE 2:24).

With the Magic Wand's Tolerance set at 0 and Anti-aliased left unchecked, I clicked on the lightest gray value and chose Similar from the Select menu. Using the Color Picker, I selected a bright orange, then pressed Option+Delete to fill the selection (FIGURE 2:25). I repeated this process for each of the gray levels, choosing colors with values that roughly corresponded to

FIGURE 2:24

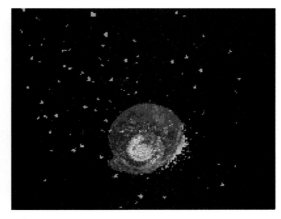

FIGURE 2:25

the values of the selected gray levels (**FIGURE 2:26**). After I finished coloring the nine gray levels, I could reselect and fine-tune colors if necessary.

FINAL PASTING

When the coloring was finished, I selected the shell again by clicking on its background with the Magic Wand, and then inverted the resulting selection. I then copied and pasted the shell onto the leaf. While the shell was a floating selection, I positioned it by clicking and dragging on the *inside* of the selection.

Once the shell was in position, I used the Curves, Levels, and Color Balance tools to adjust the shell's color in relation to the

FIGURE 2:26

leaf background. I also had the option of making the shell transparent using Composite Controls, under the Edit menu (if you are using 2.0, this menu item is called Paste Controls). You can specify a level of opacity from 1 percent to 100 percent. I entered 80% for the shell and clicked OK. Composite Controls works only with floating selections.

Before I continued to color and paste the other objects, I saved the shell's selection so that I could access it later if further corrections were necessary. To save the selection I opened the Paths palette by choosing Show Paths from the Window menu. I then clicked and dragged on the arrow in the upper-right corner of the palette and chose Make Path from the pop-up menu. This turned the shell's selection into a Pen Path, which could then be saved (see **FIGURE 2:27**, *Saving Selections*). The other objects were colored and pasted in a similar fashion but with variations in transparency and coloring (**FIGURE 2:28**).

SETTING TYPE

The final step in the Photoshop portion of the illustration was coloring the letterforms. The black *Z* was very straightforward. With the foreground color set at black, I selected the Type tool and then clicked on the illustration approximately where I wanted the letter to be. The Type Tool dialog box appeared (**FIGURE 2:29**). I chose Lithos Regular from the pop-up menu to the right of Font, and entered 120

Saving Selections

Once you have deselected (Command+D) a selection, the selection is lost, which can be a problem if you have spent some time making the selection. Photoshop provides two ways to save a selection. A selection can be made into either a path or a mask and then saved. Masks have purposes other than just for saving selections, which will be discussed in Chapter Four. They also take up a significant amount of disk space, while paths take virtually no space.

If you are using Photoshop 2.0, you save selections as paths by choosing Make Path from the Select menu, which launches the Pen program. You can then save the selection as a path by choosing Save Path from the Pen menu. Once the path has been saved, you can turn it back into a selection

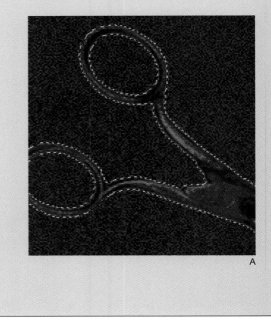

A

by clicking once inside of the path. Activate saved paths by choosing the Load Path pop-up menu from the Selection menu.

To save a selection as a path using Photo-shop 2.5:

1. Make a selection (FIGURE A). If the Paths palette is not active, choose Show Paths from the Window menu.
2. Click and drag on the arrow in the upper-right corner of the Paths palette. A pop-up menu appears. Choose Make Path (FIGURE B).
3. A dialog box will appear that allows you to set the path's Tolerance. The default setting is 2 and the range is from 0.5 to 10.0. Decreasing the Tolerance increases the number of control points used to make the path (FIGURE C). If you de-crease the Tolerance, it will take longer to make the path. If you are using Photo-shop 2.0, the Path Tolerance is set in General Preferences under the File menu.
4. When you click OK, the selection is turned into a path. You can now save the path by clicking on the arrow in the right corner of the Paths palette and choosing Save Path from the pop-up menu. Each path that you save is listed alphabeti-cally in the Paths palette (FIGURE D). Clicking on any of the listed paths acti-vates that path, which can then be made into a selection by choosing Make Selec-tion from the pop-up menu. The active path is checked.

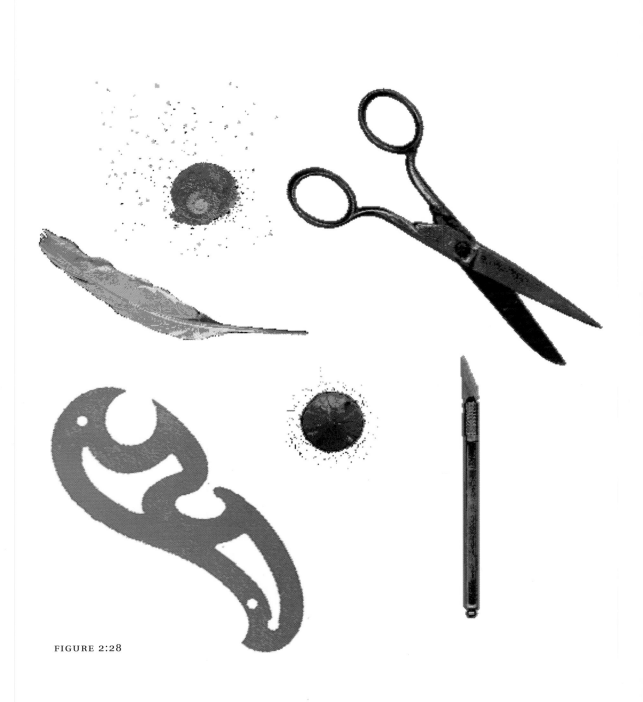

FIGURE 2:28

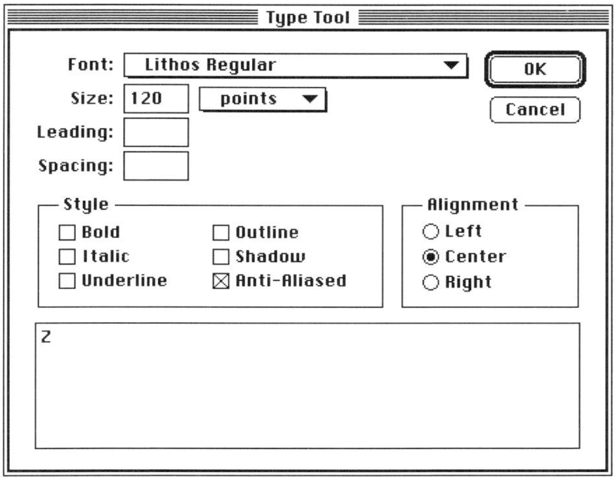

![Type Tool dialog box. Font: Lithos Regular. Size: 120 points. Leading and Spacing fields empty. Style section with checkboxes: Bold, Italic, Underline, Outline, Shadow, Anti-Aliased (checked). Alignment: Left, Center (selected), Right. Text box contains "Z". OK and Cancel buttons.]

FIGURE 2:29

points in the Size box. I also checked Anti-aliased. This ensures that the letter will be as smooth as possible given the current image resolution; you must have Adobe Type Manager installed for this to work. I entered an uppercase *Z* in the text box at the bottom and clicked OK.

The *Z* appears as a floating selection, filled with the foreground color. If the type is not exactly what you want, press Delete, click on the image again, and enter new values in the dialog box. The rules of floating selections apply—that is, once it is deselected, the type is permanently pasted. In this case I positioned the type and then made it 60 percent transparent using Composite Controls. The *Q* and *K* were set on a transparent blended rectangle and then manipulated with the painting tools (see **FIGURE 2:30**, *Q and K*).

 Because type is permanently pasted once it is deselected, setting more than a few characters at a time is very cumbersome with Photoshop. If you want to set complex type, it is often better to set the type in Adobe Illustrator and then import it into Photoshop (see Chapter Three, Importing from Illustrator*).*

Q and K

I created the *Q* and *K* letters with a combination of the Type, Blend, and Painting tools:

1. First I made a rectangular selection using the Rectangular Marquee selection tool.

2. Then I selected a foreground and background color—bright violet and aqua green in this case (FIGURE A).

A

3. I adjusted the Opacity in the Brushes palette to 50% by typing 5 (the Opacity setting in the Brushes palette affects the transparency of a blend). Then I double-clicked on the Blend tool to display a dialog box that allowed me to choose Blend Tool Options. I made the Type Linear and the Midpoint Skew 50%, then clicked OK (FIGURE B).

B

4. After clicking at the top of the selection, I dragged down to the bottom of the selection and released the mouse button. The selection was filled with a blend of the foreground color at the top and background color at the bottom (FIGURE C).

C

5. Next I changed the foreground color to bright orange, then chose Stroke from the Edit menu. I entered 1 pixel in the Width box, and 70% in the Opacity box, and clicked OK (FIGURE D).

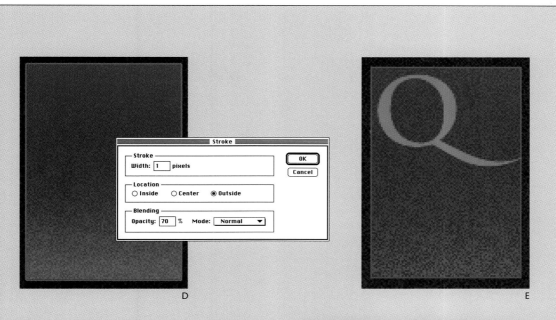

D

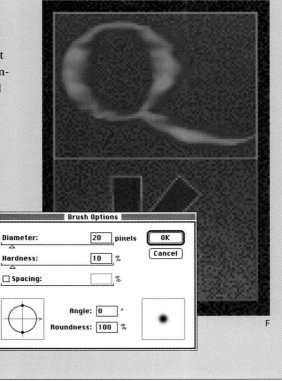

E

6. I double-clicked on the Type tool and set a Trajan Bold *Q* at 90 points. I positioned it at the top of the blended box (FIGURE E).

7. I changed the foreground color to dark violet and set a 70 point Lithos Bold *K*. I chose Composite Controls from the Edit menu, entered 65% in the Opacity box, and clicked OK.

8. I gave the *K* a 1 point stroke at 60% opacity.

9. I clicked on the Smudge tool, then double-clicked on a medium brush in the Brushes palette and entered a Diameter of 20 pixels and a Hardness of 10, and unchecked the Spacing box. I set the Opacity to 70%. Clicking and dragging on the *Q* "smudges" the pixels (FIGURE F).

F

The Brushes Palette

The Brushes palette has been greatly improved in Photoshop 2.5. You can now create an almost infinite variety of brushes and at much larger sizes—up to 999 pixels in diameter. Clicking on the arrow in the upper right-hand corner accesses a pop-up menu (FIGURE A) that allows you to customize your brushes:

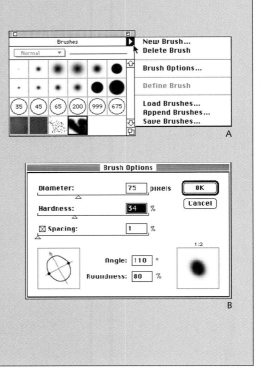

• Double-clicking on a brush or clicking once on a brush and choosing Brush Options allows you to adjust a brush stroke's diameter, hardness, spacing, angle, and roundness (FIGURE B).
• Choosing New Brush allows you to add a new brush to the palette. Delete Brush deletes the selected brush.
• Define Brush creates a brush from any currently selected pixels. This option is available only if there is an active selection.
• You can customize your Brushes palette, then save the customized palette by choosing Save Brushes. Then, to select a specific palette that you have saved, choose Load Brushes from the Brushes palette.

BRUSHES

Photoshop's painting tools are straightforward. The Pencil tool allows you to make hard-edged strokes, the Brush tool paints a soft-edged stroke, and the Airbrush tool creates an even softer edge. The Smudge tool acts like a finger on wet paint, mixing the colored pixels together. The Blur tool softens edges without mixing color (if you double-click on the Blur tool you can switch it to the Sharpening tool). Adobe has expanded the variety of possible brushes with Photoshop 2.5. The painting options can be accessed now only from the floating Brushes palette. If you are using version 2.0 you can double-click on any of the painting tools to access the Brushes palette. See FIGURE 2:31 for an overview of the new Brushes palette.

I converted the finished illustration to CMYK mode (see Chapter Seven) and exported it to Adobe Illustrator, where I added the hard-edged drawing of tools and letterforms that floats on the spine. For more information on exporting Photoshop art to other programs, see Appendices B, *File Management*, and C, *Exporting to Illustrator*.

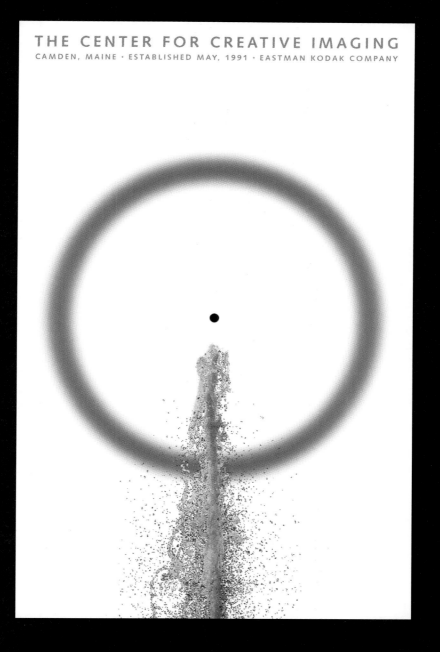

Poster for Kodak's Center for Creative Imaging, Lance Hidy © 1991

Tadanori Yokoo, Lance Hidy ©1992

Transfigure, Carl Sesto

Baseball the Great North American Game,
Published by Creative Education, Illustrations by Rob Day

3

IMPORT FROM ILLUSTRA

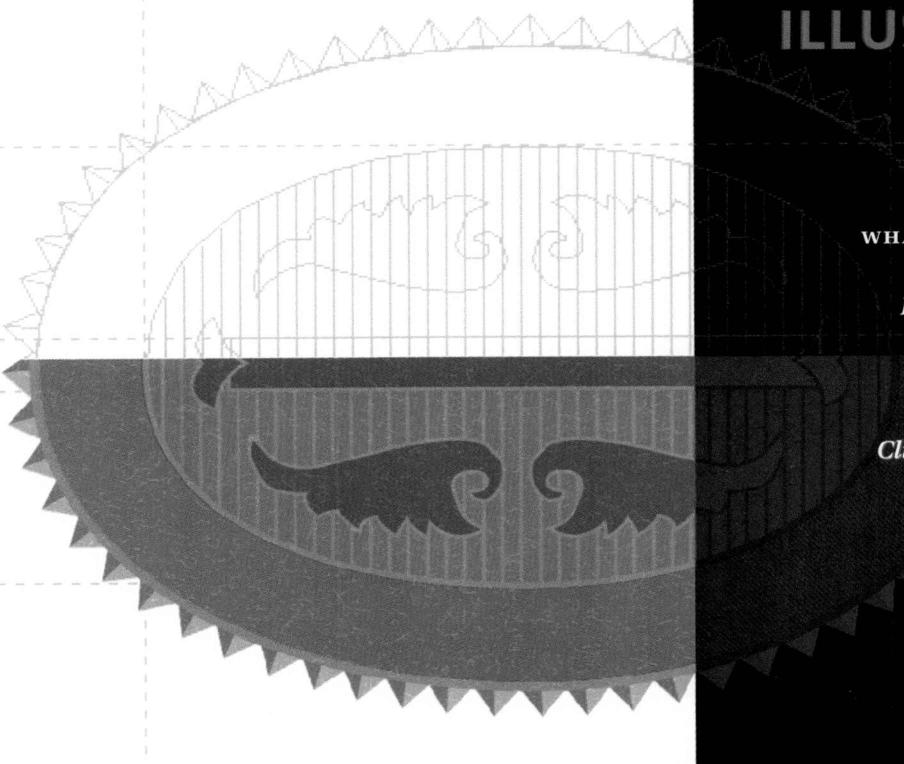

WHAT'S INSI

Resolution

Templates

Clipping Path

Placing

Opening

Trapping

As POWERFUL AS PHOTOSHOP is at manipulating continuous-tone images, it can be very cumbersome if you want to create precise, flat color images with complex typographic elements. It is, however, quite easy to import Adobe Illustrator drawings into Photoshop. You can open an Illustrator file at any resolution as a grayscale, RGB, or CMYK color file. The imported Illustrator drawing is translated from object-oriented bezier curves into color or grayscale bitmaps at any desired resolution. Once an Illustrator file is bit-mapped in Photoshop, you can manipulate it the same way you would any scanned image.

If you are an Aldus Freehand user, you must first translate your files into Adobe Illustrator format to open them in Photoshop. Altsys makes a utility called EPS Exchange that will convert Freehand files into Illustrator format. When you import Illustrator files into Photoshop, all the rules of scanned images apply; one to two pixels per halftone dot in most cases is enough to render sharp edges. If you have grown tired of the flatness associated with computer drawing programs, you can use Photoshop to add texture to the flat color. You can also combine the Illustrator drawings with photographs or artwork.

You should avoid importing finely detailed line art or typographic elements that are 100 percent of a color on a white background, if their edge appearance is important. Photoshop anti-aliases the edges of the drawing when it is bitmapped. Anti-aliasing adds pixels of intermediate color to the edge of shapes to prevent stair-stepping. Solid colors that are on light backgrounds tend to develop a fringe of halftoning, which is not desirable. (See **FIGURE 3:1,** *Imported Illustrator Resolution).*

Photoshop also has some printing advantages over Illustrator. Complex Illustrator files that use multiple blends are renowned for choking imagesetters. If I am printing a particularly complex Illustrator file, I will export it to Photoshop before outputting it on an imagesetter. The file size may increase, but because the image is bitmapped rather than object-oriented, the imagesetter has an easier time outputting the file. Photoshop also allows you to automatically trap images when they are converted to CMYK mode; if you have ever attempted to trap complex drawings in Illustrator, you can appreciate how much time this will save.

Imported Illustrator Resolution

The rules for choosing resolution when importing from Illustrator are generally the same as for scanned continuous-tone images. The art should have between one and two pixels per halftone dot. However, you should avoid type and line art on a white background. FIGURE A shows the original Illustrator file; FIGURES B, C, and D show the imported Illustrator file separated out of Photoshop at resolutions of 150, 225, and 300 ppi, respectively.

A

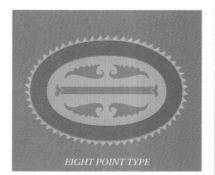

B

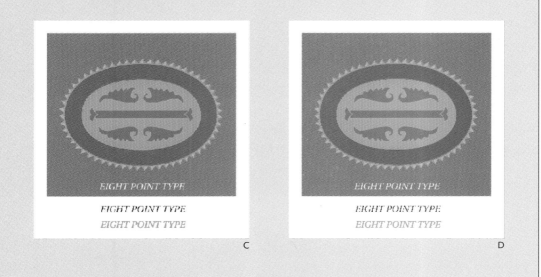

C

D

Because Photoshop's trapping is automatic, the program may not make the most desirable trap in all situations. For instance, thin, light lines on a dark background are choked rather than spread, which makes them disappear. After applying traps, always examine the image magnified to make sure there are no undesirable effects. If you are using Photoshop 2.5, you can now apply traps within a selected area.

THE BASEBALL SERIES

Creative Education of Mankato, Minnesota, commissioned our studio to design and illustrate covers for a series of children's library books on the history of each major league baseball team. The art director for the project, Rita Marshall, suggested that the illustrations bleed from the front cover across the spine to the back cover, and that they have a nostalgic look. Rita also asked that we design a logo for each of the four leagues that resembled a sticker. The titles of the books were to be integrated into these stickers.

We did not want the stickers to appear as if they had been drawn with a computer program, so rather than using perfectly flat color, we decided to add a texture that would lend to the nostalgic look of the covers. Importing the stickers into Photoshop from Illustrator allowed us to add a grainy texture to the Illustrator drawings.

PREPARING THE ILLUSTRATOR FILE

I collaborated on the sticker design with Virginia Evans, a designer and typographer. We began by making rough pencil sketches for the stickers, which we scanned and opened in Photoshop. The scans were then saved in PICT file format and opened as templates in Illustrator (see **FIGURE 3:2,** *Illustrator*

Templates). Using the templates as guides, we drew the stickers and created custom colors using Illustrator's Custom Color option. We used the custom colors rather than process color to color the drawings, so that we could globally change color later if necessary. We wanted the stickers' color to complement the color used in the Photoshop art, so it was important to be able to easily adjust each sticker's color in Illustrator before moving it into Photoshop.

 If any of the Illustrator paths are stroked or filled, and Overprint is checked in Illustrator's Paint Style dialog box, the fills and strokes may appear as a different color when the art is opened as a CMYK *file in Photoshop. For example, a 100 percent magenta fill, with Overprint checked, on top of a 75 percent yellow fill, will appear as magenta in Illustrator, but in Photoshop the magenta appears as bright orange (which is the way it will print from either program). White strokes or fills that are overprinted will disappear entirely in Photoshop.*

If you are using Photoshop 2.0, Illustrator files must be saved in a proper format before they can be opened in Photoshop. The first time you save an Illustrator file, the Save dialog box gives you these Preview options (**FIGURE 3:3**):

- None (Omit EPSF Header)
- None (Include EPSF Header)
- Black&White Macintosh
- Color Macintosh
- IBM PC

If the file is to be opened in Photoshop 2.0, choose None (Include EPSF Header) as the Preview option. If you are using Photoshop 2.5, any of the above formats will work. Black&White Macintosh and Color Macintosh previews will also work for exporting to Photoshop. These formats are for specifying either

Illustrator Templates

You can greatly improve the appearance and detail of Illustrator templates if you properly prepare them in Photoshop. Below is the sequence I use for creating a template from a sketch. This method is particularly effective if you want to use a photograph as a template.

1. Make the scan of the sketch or photograph at about 1 MB (FIGURE A). Illustrator templates can be no more than 72 ppi, so if you want the template to span the entire eighteen inch Illustrator drawing area, the scan should be 1.6 MB. In this case we made the template eight inches wide. I like to make the template large so there is more detail. After the Illustrator drawing is completed, the finished art can be reduced as necessary.

2. Choose Levels and exaggerate the contrast (FIGURE B).

3. Choose Image Size from the Image menu. Uncheck File Size, and enter the desired width—eight inches in this case. Enter a resolution of 72 pixels/inch. Click OK (FIGURE C).

4. Choose Bitmap from the Mode menu and check Diffusion Dither. Click OK and leave Input and Output at 72 pixels/inch (FIGURE D).

5. Save the file as a PICT File (FIGURE E). If you are using version 2.0, you will be prompted to choose a bit depth; choose 1 bit/pixel and click OK. Illustrator templates cannot show more than 1 bit per pixel.

6. Open Adobe Illustrator, open a New file, and choose the PICT file you have just created as a template (FIGURE F).

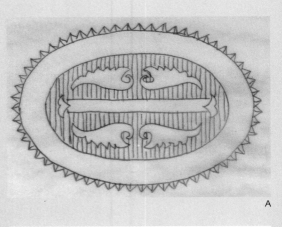

A

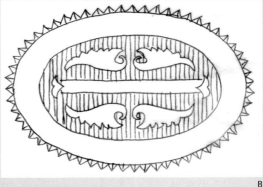

B

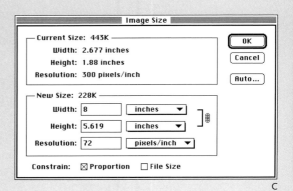

C

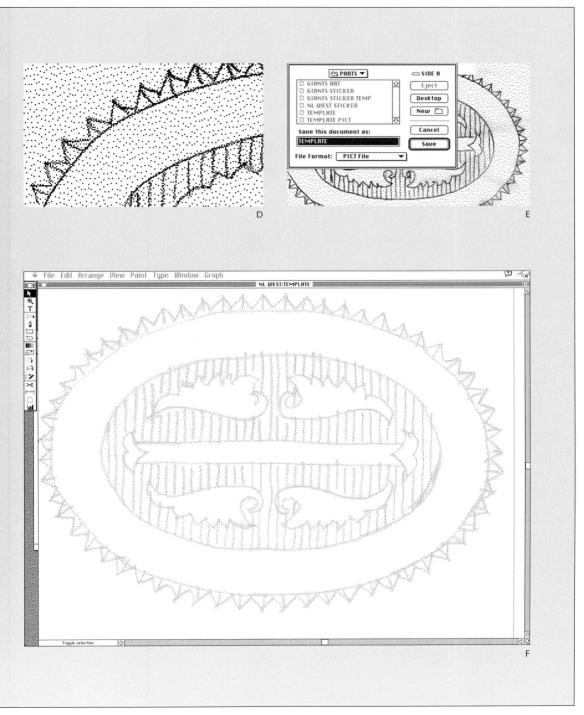

D

E

F

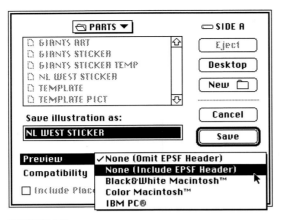

FIGURE 3:3

a color or black-and-white preview when you export Illustrator files to other programs (they will not affect the file's appearance when you import it into Photoshop). If you have already saved the file and you want to change the Preview option, choose Save As from the File menu; change the Preview option and click OK. When you are prompted to Replace Existing File, click Replace.

MIXING RESOLUTION

Because the Photoshop illustrations had to be dimensionally large (16.5"x 11") and I had 26 illustrations to create, working at full resolution was not practical. So, I decided to work at 65 ppi, which meant a file size of 2.25 MB. At this resolution, the grain of the pixels actually helped to create the nostalgic effect we were seeking.

The low resolution was perfect for the illustration, but was not high enough to maintain the kind of detail I wanted in the stickers. When I attempted to place the stickers, the 65 ppi of the Photoshop file made them appear too coarse. I solved this problem by increasing the resolution of the Photoshop illustration to accommodate more detail in the stickers. The Photoshop art had been completed, so the only work that remained was the placement and color correction of the sticker, which would not take much time even at the larger file size.

 Another method I could have used to solve the multiple-resolution problem was to create a clipping path for the sticker and then export the illustration and the textured sticker separately to Illustrator for output (see **FIGURE 3:4,** *Clipping Paths). I decided against this method because I wanted to carefully control the color relationship between the artwork and the sticker, and this was easier if I pasted the sticker directly into the illustration.*

After I increased the image resolution of the Photoshop illustration, yet another problem cropped up—the edges of the pixels became blurred, which I did not like (**FIGURE 3:5**). To solve this new problem I opened Photoshop's Preferences file by choosing General from the Preferences submenu in the File menu, and switched the interpolation method from Bicubic to Nearest Neighbor, then clicked OK (**FIGURE 3:6**). Next, I chose Image Size from the Image menu, and with File Size unchecked, I doubled the resolution to 130 ppi and clicked OK.

 The Interpolation method determines how Photoshop adds or subtracts pixels when you change an image's resolution or size. It also takes effect when you scale, rotate, skew, distort, or change perspective. It takes the computer longer to perform bicubic interpolations, but they are almost always more accurate in that they preserve the appearance of edges more accurately than the other two methods. Mixing resolutions is an exception for which you should use Nearest Neighbor. Don't forget to switch the Preferences file back to Bicubic after you use Nearest Neighbor.

Clipping Paths

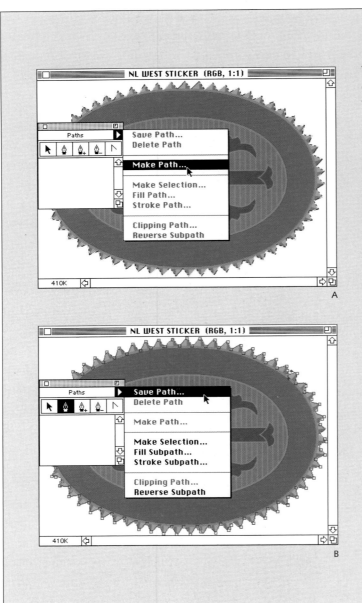

A

B

When you export Photoshop art to another program, it must be contained within a square or rectangle unless you create a *clipping path*. The clipping path allows you to import a silhouetted shape or shapes from Photoshop. The sequence for creating a clipping path has changed with Photoshop 2.5, and is described below. If you are still using Photoshop 2.0, consult your *Adobe Photoshop User Guide* for details.

1. Use the Pen Tool (from the Paths palette under the Window menu) to select the edges of the object or objects to be clipped. If you use the other selection tools, choose Make Path from the Paths palette's pop-up menu after making a selection (FIGURE A).

2. Choose Save Path from the Paths palette's pop-up menu, enter a name (FIGURE B), and click OK.

3. Choose Clipping Path from the Paths palette's pop-up menu. A Clipping Path dialog box will appear that allows you to choose the path that you want to act as the clipping path, as well as its attributes (FIGURE C). Click on Path to get a list of

C

D

all the paths that you have saved in the file. You can choose only one path to act as the clipping path. When you choose the clipping path, you can also choose a Flatness setting. You have to worry about flatness only if you are using particularly long curved segments in the path—if you are, increase the flatness to between 3 and 10; this will make it easier for the imagesetter to output the file. If you are using a very complex path—that is, a path that overlaps itself or has sub-paths—then you must choose between Even-Odd Fill Rule and Non-Zero Winding Fill Rule in order to get the clipping path to properly clip the de-sired parts of an image. The icons in the Clipping Path dialog box show how the sub-paths will clip for each method. When you have made your choices, click OK.

4. To include the clipping path with the file when you export it to another program, you must save the file in EPS format. When you open the file in another program, all of the areas outside of the clipping path will preview and print as transparent (FIGURE D). I recommend that you do not resize or distort a clipped image in another program. This will slow down the printing, and in some cases will make the file unprintable.

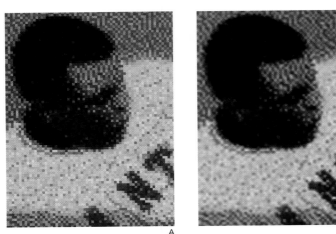

FIGURE 3:5

Figure (B) shows the fuzzy results when a pixelated image's resolution is increased using Bicubic Interpolation in the General Preferences dialog box.

By doubling the resolution using Nearest Neighbor, each image pixel is divided into four pixels of the same color, so even though I doubled the resolution, the appearance of the image did not change and I could now paste the higher resolution sticker on the lower resolution background. This method works only if the resolution is multiplied by factors of two (2, 4, 8, 16…). If I had desired, I could have increased the resolution four times, to 260 ppi. With the Photoshop illustration at 130 ppi, the file size increased to 8.75 MB. The sticker could now be imported with more detail.

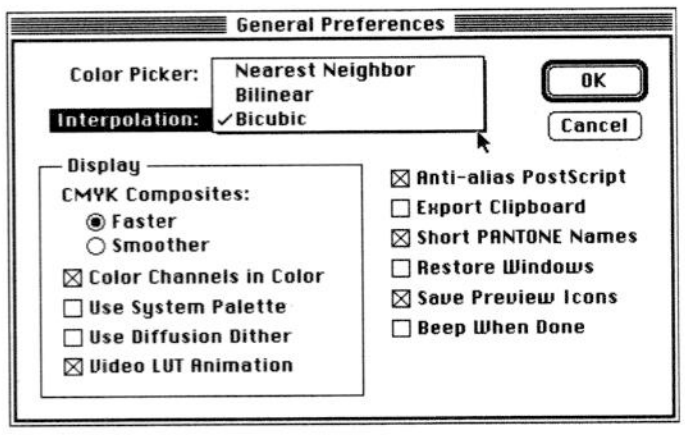

FIGURE 3:6

PLACING THE STICKER

You can import an Illustrator file by opening it as you would any Photoshop file. When you open an Illustrator drawing in Photoshop, the EPS Rasterizer dialog box appears, which allows you to choose the color mode and image resolution of the imported file. When you click OK, a new window opens that contains the Illustrator art on a white background.

You can also choose Place from the File menu to open an Illustrator file. When you use Place, the Illustrator art is opened as a floating selection in the active window. Only the drawn elements show up as floating selections—Illustrator's drawing area remains transparent.

To place an Illustrator drawing using Photoshop 2.5:

1. Choose Place from the File menu.

2. An open dialog box appears, allowing you to choose your Illustrator art. Find the art and double-click on it, or click Open.

3. An empty box with an x through it appears and then a few seconds later a preview of the Illustrator art appears inside of the box (**FIGURE 3:7**). You can now ma-

nipulate the preview's size, proportions, and position before placing a full-resolution version of the art.

4. Clicking and dragging on any of the corners of the preview will resize the art while constraining its proportions. If you want to distort the art, hold down the Command key while dragging the corner (**FIGURE 3:8**). To delete the preview, click once outside of the box.

5. When the cursor is on the x inside of the preview box it turns to a pointer; clicking and dragging on the x moves the art. When the cursor is anywhere else inside of the box it turns to a gavel (**FIGURE 3:9**); clicking once with the gavel places the finished high-resolution art (**FIGURE 3:10**).

FIGURE 3:7

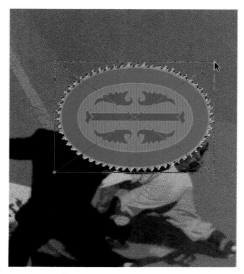

FIGURE 3:8

FIGURE 3:10

IMPORTED COLOR

When you place or open an Illustrator file in RGB mode, its color in Photoshop will vary depending on what is entered in Monitor Setup and Printing Inks Setup in Photoshop's Preferences submenu under the File menu. To get the colors you specify in Illustrator to be the same in Photoshop:

1. Open an Illustrator file that contains a wide variety of color, as a CMYK file in Photoshop.

2. Open the same file in Illustrator and compare its preview to the Photoshop preview.

3. Change the Dot Gain percentage and Gray Balance in the Custom dialog box of the Printing Inks Setup until the Photoshop preview matches the Illustrator preview.

4. When you come close to matching the previews, save the Printing Inks Setup and load it before placing Illustrator art into RGB Photoshop files (see Chapter Seven, *Saving Calibration Settings*).

It is also possible to match Illustrator's CMYK color patches to Photoshop's digitally. Open Photoshop's General Preferences under File, and choose Apple as the Color Picker. Then choose Printing Inks Setup from the Preferences menu and choose Custom from the Ink Colors pop-up menu. Click on each color patch and record its RGB values. Then open Illustrator and choose Progressive Colors from its Preferences dialog box. Click on each color patch and enter the RGB values that you recorded from Photoshop. If you are working with a calibrated monitor, this method will make your *displayed* Illustrator color more accurate; it will also change the displayed color of any existing drawings.

When the sticker was sized and positioned properly, I rotated and color-corrected it, and then added some noise to give it texture. I chose Add Noise from the Noise submenu under Filter, entered 18 in the Amount box, and clicked OK (**FIGURE 3:11**).

Before I deselected and pasted the sticker, I made and saved a path of the selection by choosing Make Path, then Save Path from the Paths palette. With the path saved, it could easily be reselected later. Finally, I color-corrected the sticker in relationship to the illustration using Levels and Color Balance, found in the Adjust submenu under Image (**FIGURE 3:12**).

When the illustration was complete, I converted it to CMYK (see Chapter Seven) and then exported the entire illustration back to Illustrator, where the type was set and crop marks were created. For more information on exporting Photoshop files to Illustrator, see Appendix C, *Exporting to Illustrator*.

FIGURE 3:11

FIGURE 3:12

Saxo Player, Javier Romero ©1991 Javier Romero Design Inc.

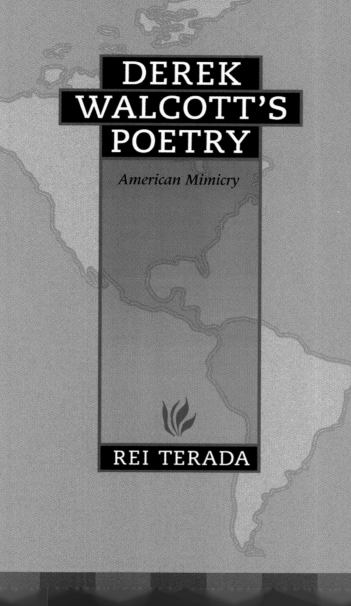

DEREK WALCOTT'S POETRY

American Mimicry

REI TERADA

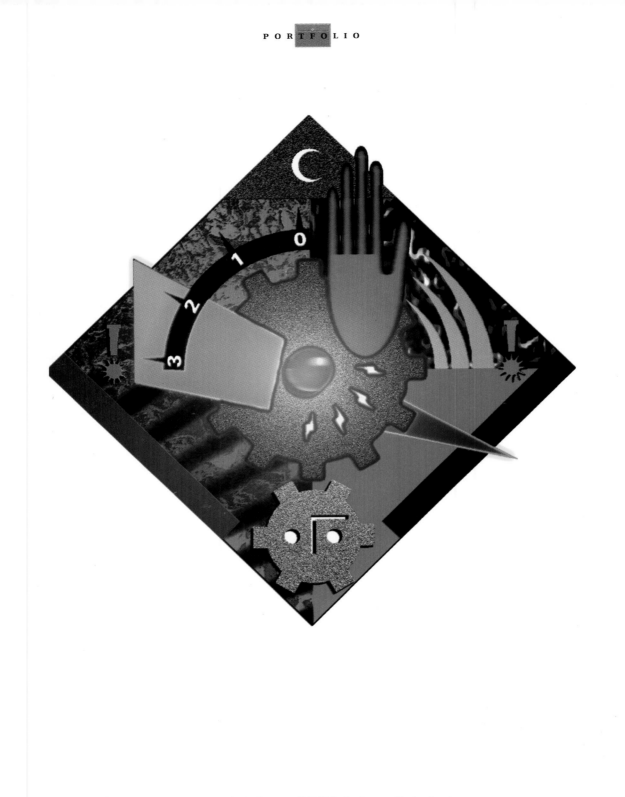

Mystic, Javier Romero ©1991 Javier Romero Design Inc.

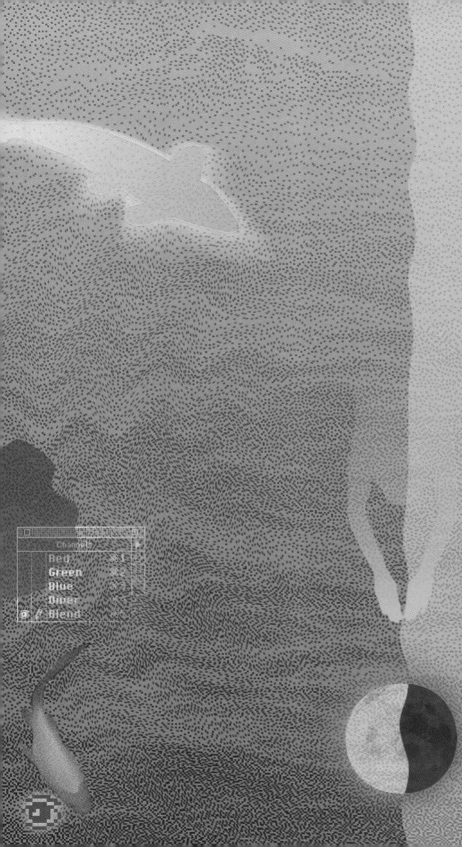

4
MASKS

■   ■   ■

Masks are a sophisticated way of controlling and manipulating specific areas of an image. They can be used for straightforward tasks such as saving a selection that has been time-consuming to create, or they can be used for more complex image editing tasks. With masks, you can create subtle blends and color shifts within images, or regulate how a filter affects a specific part of an image. When Photoshop was first released, masks were called *alpha channels*. Version 2.0 dropped the term alpha channel for the more user-friendly Save Selection and Load Selection, but you may still hear the term alpha channel used.

There are analogies in traditional graphic arts to Photoshop's masks. Printers use rubyliths to mask or silhouette photographs and art when preparing them for reproduction. Silkscreen printing provides another analogy in the way it employs masks or stencils to block parts of a screen and leave other parts open for ink to pass through onto paper. Photoshop 2.5 has a new tool that bears an even closer resemblance to rubyliths, called Quick Masks, which are temporary channels described in detail later in this chapter.

CHANNELS

Every RGB Photoshop file has three channels, one for each of the RGB colors, and a full-color preview that you use for editing the image (**FIGURE 4:1**). If you select part of the image, the selection can be saved as a mask by choosing Save Selection from the Selection menu. When you save a selection, a new grayscale channel is added to the three RGB channels (**FIGURE 4:2**). The white areas of the new channel represent the saved selection, and the black areas are the mask (think of the white areas as the cut-away parts of a rubylith, or the open areas in a silkscreen). The addition of the new channel increases the file

FIGURE 4:1

FIGURE 4:2

size. A 3 MB RGB file becomes 4 MB when a channel is added because each of the RGB channels and the new channel are 1 MB, or a third of the original file size.

If you are using Photoshop 2.5, there is a new floating palette called Channels that is accessed from the Window menu (see **FIGURE 4:3,** *The Channels Palette*). This new palette makes it easier to view and manage saved masks. You can Delete, Merge, and Split channels from the Channels palette; in Photoshop 2.0, these items were found under the Mode menu.

After you make a selection, it can be saved as a new channel by choosing Save Selection from the Selection menu. If you are using Photoshop 2.0, the resulting new channel is previewed. If you are using version 2.5, the channel in which you made the selection—usually RGB—remains the preview. Each new channel you create is assigned a number. If you are working in RGB mode, the red, green, and blue channels are always numbered 1, 2, and 3, respectively, and new channels are numbered in order of their creation, starting with the number 4.

The Channels Palette

The Channels palette's pop-up menu (FIGURE A) allows you to manage a file's channels. Choosing New Channel adds a new, blank channel to the file. Delete Channel removes the channel currently being viewed (you cannot delete the master RGB channel).

When you first save a selection, the resulting channel is added to the Channels list and assigned a number. When you are viewing a chan-

nel, Channel Options is available. Choosing Channel Options gives you a dialog box that allows you to rename the channels you have created (FIGURE B). You can also assign a Color and Opacity to the previews of saved channels so that when you view two or more channels at once they appear as color overlays—the default is 55% orange. The opacity of the channel's overlay color has no affect on the channel's function

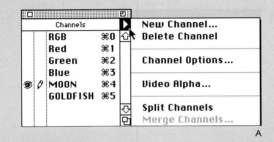

A

B

as a mask when it is loaded as a selection. Clicking once on the color box in this dialog box calls up the Color Picker, which allows you to change the currently viewed channel's overlay color.

FIGURE C shows the Moon and Goldfish channels viewed as overlays. You can click and Shift-click on the Eye icons at the left of the palette to view any combination of the channels

as overlays. FIGURE D shows the Moon overlayed with the RGB channel. You can also Shift-click the pencil icons to write-protect any of the channels. If the pencil icon shows with all of the channels, then any operation performed affects all of the channels even when the preview is RGB. Clicking on a channel's title previews that channel.

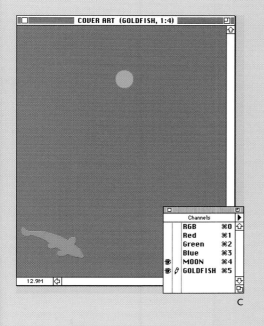

C

D

When you preview a channel, the channel's number appears to the left of the size ratio in the title bar. The individual channels are easily viewed by pressing Command plus the channel's number. The red, green, and blue channels are Command+1, 2, and 3, respectively; the first saved selection is Command+4, the next is Command+5, and so on (**FIGURE 4:4**). To return to the RGB preview, type Command+0. You can also preview any channel by clicking on its name or number in the Paths palette.

The simplest use of a mask is saving a selection that is made manually, so that it can be reloaded anytime after it has been deselected. However, because masks add considerable size to a file, using them for this purpose can make a large file unmanageable. A better way to save a manual selection is to use the Pen tool to make the selection, and then save the selection as a path (see Chapter Two, *2.5's Paths Palette*). You can also convert a selection made with any of the other selection tools into a Pen path by choosing Make Path from the Paths palette, and then saving the path. Saving a path does not increase the size of a file, and there is no limit to the number of paths you can save (you can save only sixteen masks in one document).

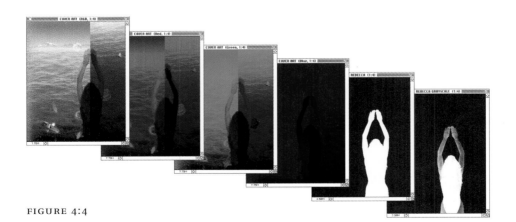

FIGURE 4:4

If you convert a complex selection made by the Magic Wand or Lasso tool to a path and save it, then load the path and convert it back to a selection, the resulting selection will not be identical to the original selection. If you need a selection to be saved perfectly, pixel-for-pixel, you should save it as a selection, not a path.

DESIGNER PHOTOSHOP'S COVER

I used a number of masking techniques when I created the illustration for the cover of this book. Because the illustration is so complex, I'll only explain the techniques that relate to masking. The illustration was created using six masking techniques:

- Creating a blend within an image
- Quick Masks
- Using gray scales as masks
- Filters through masks
- Drop shadows and glows
- Fade outs

You should master the basic skills of cutting, pasting, and resizing covered in Chapter Two before attempting masks.

BLENDS AS MASKS

I started the illustration with a photograph of water that I scanned on a Nikon LS-3500 slide scanner (**FIGURE 4:5**). I cropped the scan to the trim size of the cover (7.375"x 9.25") at a resolution of 200 ppi, which produced a file size of 7.75 MB (see Chapter One, FIGURE 1:16 *Accurate Scanning*). The water is the background for the illustration, and the other elements are pasted onto it in various ways using masks.

FIGURE 4:5

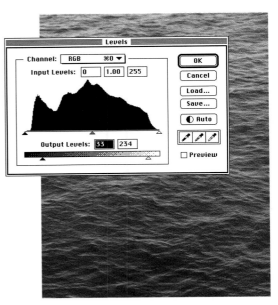

FIGURE 4:6

I wanted the water to have more depth, so first I lowered its contrast with Levels (Command+L) by moving the Output sliders toward each other (**FIGURE 4:6**). Adjusting the overall contrast of the water did not give the effect that I was looking for, so I decided to change the contrast and value of the water gradually from bottom to top. To accomplish this effect, I created a blend in a new channel and loaded the blend as a selection. To graduate the contrast:

1. I created a new channel by choosing New Channel from the Channels palette.

2. With the foreground and background colors set to black and white, respectively, I double-clicked on the Blend tool (clicking once on the miniature Color Picker icon at the bottom of the tool box returns the Color Picker to its defaults).

FIGURE 4:7

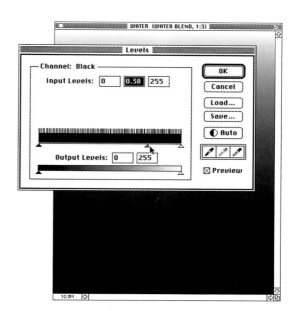

FIGURE 4:8

3. I specified a Linear Blend, with a Midpoint Skew of 50% and a style of Normal (the Blend tool's defaults). Starting from the bottom, I dragged the cursor to the top (**FIGURE 4:7**). The percentage that I specified as the Midpoint Skew determined where the blend would break. Where a blend breaks can also be altered by using Levels. Open Levels and move the middle Input slider left or right, and you can adjust the break interactively (**FIGURE 4:8**).

4. Next, I added a small amount of noise to the blend. Adding noise reduces the banding that often occurs in blends. I chose Add Noise from the Noise submenu in the Filter menu and entered 7 as the Amount and Gaussian as the Distribution (**FIGURE 4:9**).

5. With the blend completed, I returned to the RGB preview and chose Load Selection from the Selection menu; this

loads the blend as a mask (**FIGURE 4:10**). If you have saved more than one selection, a list of the channels appears as a pop-up submenu to the right of Load Selection, and you can choose which channel you want to load.

6. Finally, I opened Levels and lowered the contrast and brightness by moving the left Output slider to the right and clicking OK; **FIGURE 4:11** shows the result.

When you load a mask that has grayscale elements, any operation that you perform is modified by the values of the mask's pixels. In this case, I intended to brighten and lower the contrast of the water, and because the blended mask was loaded, any adjustments occurred gradually relative to the gray values in the blend. The water was adjusted the most at the top, where the mask was solid white, and was not adjusted at all at the bottom, where the mask was solid black. In the middle of the blend, where the mask is a 50% gray value, the contrast and brightness changed half as much.

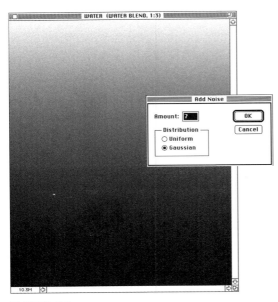

FIGURE 4:9

FIGURE 4:10

After I had adjusted the contrast of the water, I deselected the blend selection (Command+D), went back to the blend mask (Command+4), inverted it (Command+I), and adjusted the break of the blend using Levels. I returned to the RGB preview and loaded the inverted blend. Because I had inverted the blend, the open part of the mask (the white area) was now at the bottom of the water. I wanted the foreground part of the water to gradually turn violet, so I opened Color Balance from the Adjust submenu under Image (Command+Y), added Red and Magenta, and clicked OK. This tinted the foreground water violet (**FIGURE 4:12**).

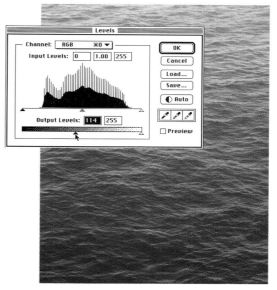

FIGURE 4:11

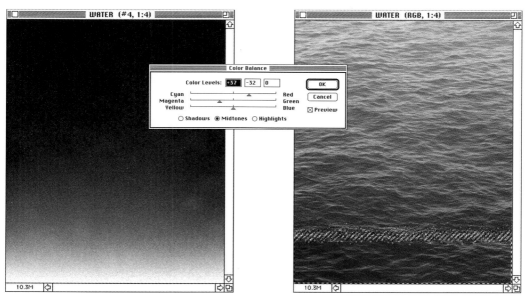

FIGURE 4:12

QUICK MASKS

Quick Masks are a new feature of Photoshop 2.5 that represent an even closer analogy to rubyliths and amberliths than saved selections. With Quick Masks you can create a temporary mask without committing it to a channel. You can also work on the mask and see the artwork at the same time—the mask acts as an overlay. This feature makes selecting easier, particularly for beginners. To use Quick Masks:

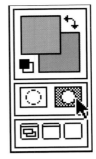

FIGURE 4:13

1. Make a selection and then click once on the right-hand Quick Mask icon in the tool box (**FIGURE 4:13**). The selection marquee disappears, and all of the nonselected areas are covered with a transparent orange overlay (**FIGURE 4:14**). If you have the Channels palette showing (choose Show Channels from the Window menu), the Quick mask is listed as a new channel titled *Mask*. A Quick Mask functions in the same way as a saved selection, except that you can see our artwork as you alter the mask.

FIGURE 4:14

FIGURE 4:15

2. Double-clicking on the Quick Mask icons displays a dialog box (**FIGURE 4:15**) that allows you to adjust the transparency and color of the overlay, and to reverse the overlay so that the colored area represents the selected area. Clicking on the color patch in this dialog box displays a Color Picker that allows you to change the overlay color.

3. When the overlay is active, it can be edited with any of the selection and painting tools as if were a grayscale channel. You can use the selection tools to select an area, then either delete that part of the overlay or fill it with the overlay color (**FIGURE 4:16**). You can also paint on the overlay color. The Color Picker shows grayscale only when a Quick Mask is active. Painting with white removes mask (**FIGURE 4:17**), black adds mask, and grays add a percentage of mask.

FIGURE 4:16

FIGURE 4:17

FIGURE 4:18

4. Once you have finished editing the overlay, click the left-hand Quick Mask icon and the edited overlay becomes a selection again (**FIGURE 4:18**).

GRAYSCALE MASKS

Masks can be more complex than simple blends and black and white selections. Any grayscale image can be used as a mask, which can be very useful for coloring grayscale images. Though it is very easy to colorize any grayscale image using the color-correcting tools, I find that with masks I can make more specific color choices and I generally have more control over the image. I used a mask to color the diver in the cover illustration in the following way:

1. I scanned the figure from a film negative and sized it to be slightly smaller than the water's trim (see **FIGURE 2:17**, *Cutting and Pasting*).

2. To select the figure, I used the Pen tool, then saved the resulting path so that I could reselect it later if necessary (**FIGURE 4:19**).

3. I made the path a selection, copied the selection, and pasted it onto the water. I saved the scan of the figure and closed the file (Command+W).

4. While it was still a floating selection, I sized the figure to the proportions that I desired, using the Scale tool (see Chapter Two, *Scaling and Rotating*).

5. Once the figure was properly sized (**FIGURE 4:20**), I wanted to make and save a path of the figure's selection, but if I had made the selection into a path, the grayscale would have been permanently pasted down, which I did not want. To solve this problem, I made a copy of the floating selection, opened a new file, and pasted the copy into the new file. I saved this new file in case I needed a copy of the resized figure later.

FIGURE 4:19

FIGURE 4:20

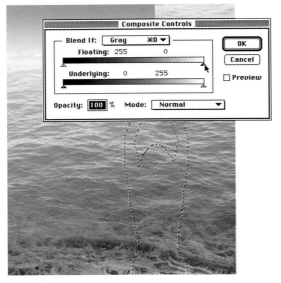

FIGURE 4:21

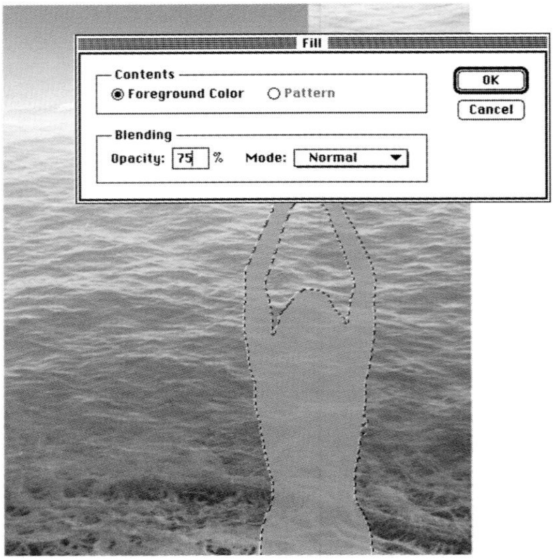

FIGURE 4:22

6. Next, I returned to the water's window, where the selection was still floating. I chose Composite Controls from the Edit menu and reversed the arrows under the grayscale bar that appears beneath Floating; this reversed the read-out at the right of Floating to 255 on the left and 0 on the right. I clicked OK. This made the floating selection completely transparent (**FIGURE 4:21**). I could now make and save the outline as a path without pasting the grayscale onto the water. I make a habit of saving any pasted object's selection as a path before permanently pasting it, because paths take up virtually no space in memory.

7. I converted the saved path back into a selection and filled the selection with a slightly transparent bright yellow. To do this, I changed the foreground color to bright yellow and then chose Fill from the Edit menu, entered an Opacity of 75%, and clicked OK (**FIGURE 4:22**).

8. After filling the figure with transparent yellow, I saved the selection and then previewed the newly saved selection (Command-5). I loaded the new selection and pasted the grayscale figure, which was

still on the clipboard, into the mask (**FIG-URE 4:23**). Because the selected white area of the mask matched the figure on the clipboard, the figure pasted perfectly into the selection. Pasted objects paste into the center of the current selection. If there is not a current selection, the object pastes into the center of the window.

9. Before deselecting the grayscale figure, I inverted it (Command+I); this made the shadow areas white (**FIGURE 4:24**). I returned to the RGB preview, and loaded the inverted grayscale as a selection (**FIGURE 4:25**).

FIGURE 4:23

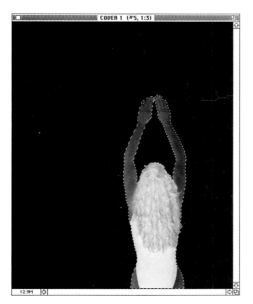

FIGURE 4:24

FIGURE 4:25

FIGURE 4:26

10. I could now fill the shadows with any color. I chose a dark violet foreground color and pressed Option+Delete to make the fill (**FIGURE 4:26**).

 You can make any floating selection transparent by choosing Composite Controls from the Edit menu and entering a percentage in the Opacity box. A shortcut for changing a floating selection's transparency is to activate one of the selection tools and then adjust Opacity in the Brushes palette.

With the path of the figure's outline saved and its grayscale saved as a mask, I had a great deal of flexibility coloring the grayscale. I could easily try different fill colors for the shadows, or I could load the path, turn it to a selection, alter the yellow, and then reload the mask of the shadow areas and try other colors. Once I had settled on a shadow color, I could load the saved path, convert it to a selection, and use the color-correction tools to fine-tune the figure's overall color and contrast.

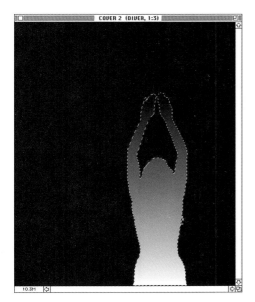

FIGURE 4:27

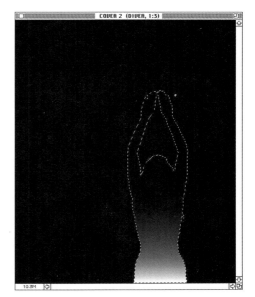

FIGURE 4:28

FILTERS THROUGH MASKS

Any fill, color correction, or filter operation that you perform
with a grayscale mask loaded is modified by the gray levels of
the mask. I wanted to blend the diver into the water seamlessly,
and to do this I applied the ZigZag filter through a blend. Below
is the sequence I used:

1. I loaded the mask of the diver and then made a Linear blend
   from black at the top white at the bottom (**FIGURE 4:27**).

2. The blend was too gradual, so I adjusted it by choosing Levels and moving the middle slider to the right, which caused
   the blend to break closer to the bottom (**FIGURE 4:28**).

3. With the blend adjusted, I chose ZigZag from the Distort
   submenu under Filter. I entered 40 as the Amount, 6 as the
   number of Ridges, and Around Center as the method, and
   clicked OK (**FIGURE 4:29**).

FIGURE 4:29

Because the blend was loaded as a mask, the ZigZag filter was applied with increasing intensity as the figure merged with the water.

 When applying a filter to an entire image, you can modify the intensity of the filter by loading a channel filled with a percentage of gray before applying the filter. If the channel is filled with 50 percent gray, the filter is applied with half as much intensity. A quick way of creating a 50 percent gray channel is to choose Constant from the Calculate submenu under Image and make the Level 128 and the Channel New.

FIGURE 4:30

DROP SHADOWS AND GLOWS

Masks can be used to create very accurate drop shadows and glows. I used a mask to create the orange glow behind the shell that floats to the left of the figure. There are many methods for creating glows and drop shadows with Photoshop.

Below is the method I use most often:

1. I scanned the shell on a flatbed scanner and selected it using the Pen tool (**FIGURE 4:30**). To create an interesting lighting effect, I used a secondary light source when I scanned the shell. Positioning a desk lamp facing into the side of the scanner, I experimented with various angles to alter the shell's lighting (**FIGURE 4:31**).

2. Before pasting the shell into the design, I loaded the figure's path and converted it to a selection. Rather than pasting the shell directly into the window, I chose Paste

FIGURE 4:31

FIGURE 4:32

FIGURE 4:33

Behind from the Edit menu. The shell was pasted as a floating selection behind the figure. I then rotated, resized, and positioned the shell. I also made the shell negative (Command+I) and color corrected it (**FIGURE 4:32**).

3. I made a path of the shell's selection and saved it (saving the path is an important step). I then converted the path to a selection and saved the resulting selection (**FIGURE 4:33**). The saved selection became Channel #6, which I re-named Shell using Channel Options in the Channels palette. Double-clicking on the name of any of the channels that you have created also calls up the Channel Options dialog box.

4. Next, I reselected the shell by choosing Shell from the Load Selection submenu. I then changed the foreground color to white by clicking on the Eyedropper tool, and then clicking on the white area of the channel. If you are using version

FIGURE 4:34

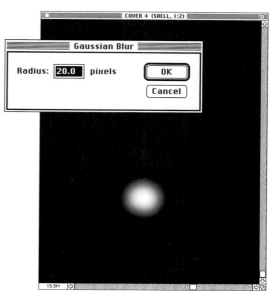

FIGURE 4:35

2.5, clicking on the Arrow icon, above the color patches in the tool box, swaps the foreground and background colors. With the foreground color white, I chose Stroke from the Edit menu and specified a Width of 10 pixels and a Location of Center, and clicked OK (**FIGURE 4:34**).

5. I deselected the shell (Command+D), and chose Gaussian Blur from the Blur submenu under Filter. Gaussian Blur allows you to specify how much a selection is blurred. I chose a Radius of 20 pixels and clicked OK (**FIGURE 4:35**).

6. I did not want the glow to be uniform, so I shifted the mask to the left and down using the Offset Filter. I chose Offset from the Other submenu under the Filter menu and entered –20 pixels right in the Horizontal box and 10 pixels down in the Vertical box. I set Undefined Areas to Repeat Edge Pixels, which ensured that the edges of the channel remained black.

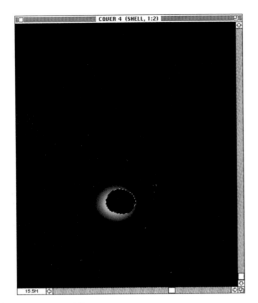

FIGURE 4:36

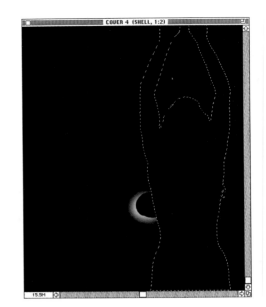

FIGURE 4:37

FIGURE 4:38

7. Next, I loaded the saved shell path and made it a selection. I clicked on the miniature Color Picker icon at the bottom of the tool box to make the foreground color black, and pressed Option+Delete to fill the shell selection with black (**FIGURE 4:36**).

8. I repeated step 7 using the figure's path (**FIGURE 4:37**).

9. Finally, I returned to the RGB preview, loaded the Shell channel, and filled it with bright orange (**FIGURE 4:38**).

If you use this method for creating drop shadows, fill the mask with a percentage of gray or open Levels and move the right Output slider halfway to the left. This darkens and lowers the contrast of the selected area, creating a realistic shadow.

FADE OUTS

Masks can be used to make one image fade into another. I used this technique to make the goldfish, swimming to the left of the shell, fade into the water. After I had created the fade out I gave the fish a subtle, blended glow and then used the ZigZag filter to create a ripple effect. To create a fade out:

1. I scanned the goldfish from a slide and then selected it with the Pen tool (**FIGURE 4:39**).

FIGURE 4:39

FIGURE 4:40

FIGURE 4:41

2. I saved the Pen path, converted the path to a selection, and then copied and pasted the goldfish into the illustration.

3. Once I had the goldfish sized and positioned properly in the illustration (**FIGURE 4:40**), I copied it (an important step), chose Composite Controls from the Edit menu, reversed the arrows under the Floating grayscale bar, and clicked OK. This made the floating fish selection completely transparent.

4. With the goldfish transparent, I made its selection into a path (**FIGURE 4:41**), saved the path, then converted the path back to a selection.

5. I saved the goldfish selection and then named it Goldfish (**FIGURE 4:42**).

6. I loaded the newly created channel by choosing Goldfish from the Load Selection submenu under Selection, and created a black-to-white radial blend from the fish's head to its tail, using white as the foreground and black as the background colors (**FIGURE 4:43**).

7. After blending the fish mask, I returned to the RGB preview and again loaded the Goldfish mask, (**FIGURE 4:44**) and chose Paste Into from the Edit menu. The fish, which was still on the clipboard, pasted into the selected blend as transparency, gradated from head to tail (**FIGURE 4:45**).

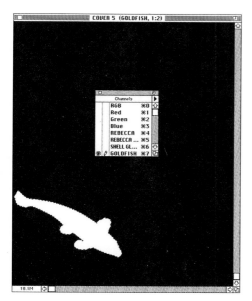

FIGURE 4:42

FIGURE 4:43

FIGURE 4:44

FIGURE 4:45

If I need to adjust the amount of a fade, I press Command+Z to undo the paste, deselect the blend (Command+D), and return to the blend channel (Command+7, in this case). I then use Levels to adjust where the blend breaks and repeat step 7 (see step 3, *Blends as Masks*).

LOADING MASKS REMOTELY

At this this point I had created four new channels in the illustration, and the file size was becoming a problem—it had more than doubled, to 18 MB. So I decided to store the masks as separate documents and load the masks remotely if I needed to use them again. This technique allows you to save as many masks as there is storage space for. Deleting masks from large files also frees up memory, which can speed operations (see Appendix D, *Faster Photoshop*).

To separate the channels from the illustration, I choose Duplicate from the Calculate menu. Then I choose the channel that I want to duplicate from the Source Channel pop-up menu, leave the Destination as New, and click OK. This creates a duplicate, untitled copy of the specified channel. I save the new file to a folder that I named MASKS, which I store in the same folder as the art work. After I have duplicated and saved each of the masks, I delete the channels by previewing the channel to be deleted, and choosing Delete Channel from the Channels palette.

If I need to load one of the saved masks into the artwork, I open the desired mask along with the artwork, and choose Duplicate from the Calculate menu. I choose the mask that I have just opened as the Source 1 Document, the artwork that I want to load the mask into as the Destination Document, and Selection as the Destination Channel (**FIGURE 4:46**). When I click OK, the mask is loaded as a selection into the artwork. I can then close the saved mask and continue to work.

FIGURE 4:46

You cannot load a channel remotely if you have changed the pixel dimensions of either the saved channel or the artwork. Settle on your final resolution and cropping before saving a channel as a separate document.

Once you have mastered the basic concepts of masking, you will have much more control over Photoshop images. The techniques described above are only a few of the possibilities. It is worth the effort to understand masks so that they become second nature.

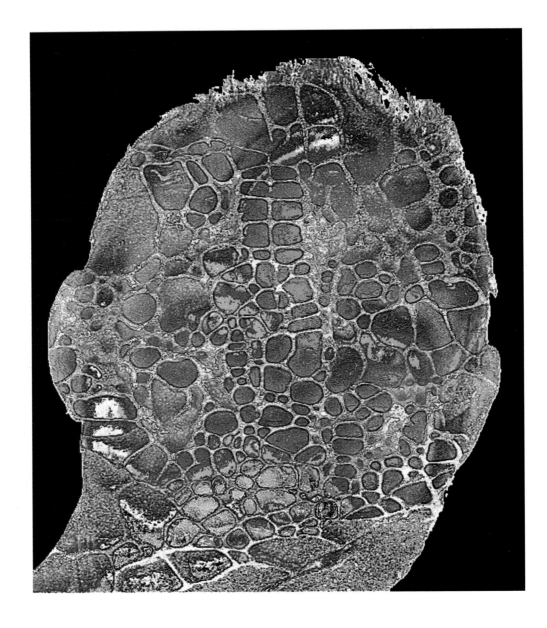

Bean Face, Sumner Stone ©1992 Stone Type Foundry Inc.

Die Altstadt, Alan Magee © 1992

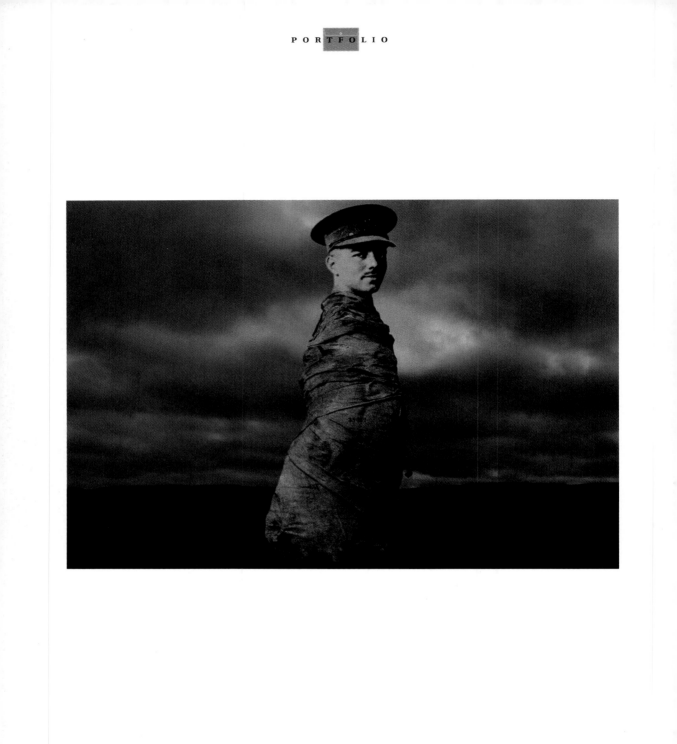

Pro Patria Mori, Alan Magee ©1992

LANCE HIDY AND I HAVE shared a Newburyport, Massachusetts, studio since 1989. Our alliance actually began ten years earlier. Lance had abandoned designing fine-art photography books to pursue a career in poster design, and I had started a fine-art screen-printing business. We collaborated on nearly 40 hand-printed editions between 1981 and 1989 for clients as diverse as Aspo/Lamaze and the Library of Congress.

Lance was one of the first designers to understand the implications of an electronic prepress system on the desktop of every designer and illustrator. While proprietary electronic prepress systems have existed for more than twenty years, artists and designers rarely had an opportunity to use them because of their $400 to $500 hourly rental fees. Not only was the cost of renting time on one of these systems prohibitive, but when artists did have access, there was always a technician between the artist and the controls.

The first version of Photoshop arrived in our studio in the spring of 1989. Even though Lance's posters were flat color screen prints, he had always used his own photographs as the basis for the art, so the idea of being able to manipulate photographs electronically was very appealing despite the output limitations at the time. Lance now designs most of his posters using Photoshop. This chapter shows how one of the leading Photoshop artists uses the program to create a personal photo montage.

CREATING THE BACKGROUND

Lance started the montage with an abstract backdrop made by manipulating a photograph of grass that he had taken. He used a combination of the Magic Wand and Unsharp Mask filter to create the backdrop.

1. First, Lance scanned the grass slide and then cropped it to the dimensions of the finished piece (see Chapter One, *Accurate Scanning*).

2. After cropping the scan, he double-clicked on the Magic Wand tool, set its Tolerance to 40 with Anti-aliased checked, and then clicked OK.

3. Next he clicked once on a highlight in the grass scan, which selected the highlight, then chose Similar from the

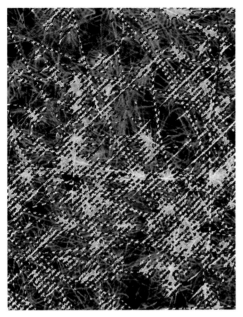

FIGURE 5:1

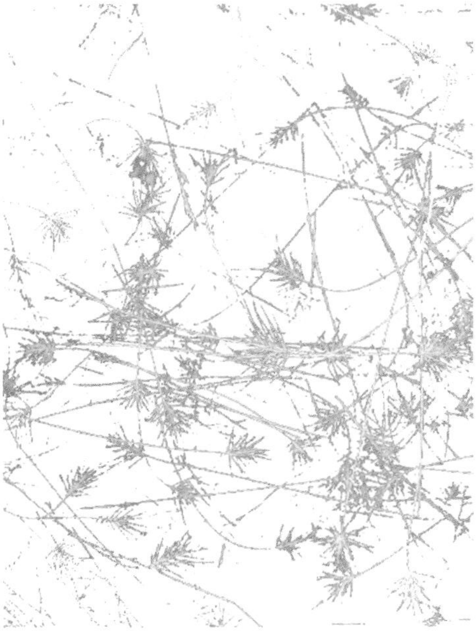

FIGURE 5:2

Select menu to select the other highlights of similar value in the image (**FIGURE 5:1**). Select Similar is affected by the Magic Wand's Tolerance setting. Increasing the Magic Wand's Tolerance increases the range of pixels added to a selection when you choose Similar.

4. Lance then inverted the selection by choosing Inverse from the Select menu, and pressed Delete to erase the shadow areas of the scan (**FIGURE 5:2**).

5. With the shadows deleted, Lance deselected the selection (Command+D) and chose Unsharp Mask from the Sharpen submenu under the Filter menu. He then entered an Amount of 200%, a Radius of 2 pixels, and a Threshold level of 1, and clicked OK. He repeated the Unsharp Mask filter three times (Command+F repeats the last filter used), which produced the effect shown in **FIGURE 5:3,** and in close-up in **FIGURE 5:4**.

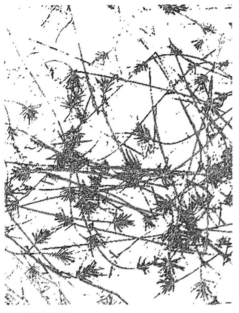

FIGURE 5:3

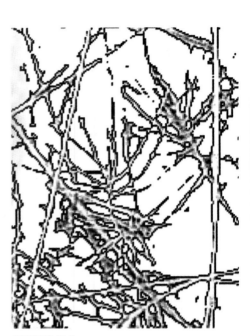

FIGURE 5:4

FEATHERING SELECTIONS

After he had finished creating the background texture, Lance
started to assemble the other elements of the montage. The
first two elements, a portrait of his father surfing taken by
Lance's mother in the mid-fifties and a statue of Buddha, were
manipulated with the help of the Feather tool under the Selection menu. In the case of the portrait, he feathered a circle selection to create a vignette. He then feathered selections of the
shadows and highlights in order to color the grayscale Buddha.
To add the portrait and Buddha to the montage:

1. Lance scanned the portrait and then resized it to fit within
   the grass window (see *Cutting and Pasting*, Chapter Two).
   He then exaggerated the sharpness of the scan by entering
   an Amount of 400%, a Radius of 2 pixels, and a Threshold
   level of 1 in the Unsharp Mask dialog box (**FIGURE 5:5**).

2. Next, Lance selected the Elliptical Marquee tool from the tool box. He held down the Option key and, clicking on the center of the scan, pulled out a circle selection. Before releasing the mouse button, he pressed the Option+Shift key, which constrained the ellipse to a circle. He then feathered the selection by choosing Feather from the Select menu and entering 15 as the Feather Radius (**FIGURE 5:6**). If you are using Photoshop 2.5, you can apply a feather before making a selection by double-clicking on the Rectangular or Elliptical selection icons and entering a Feather Radius.

FIGURE 5:5

FIGURE 5:6

FIGURE 5:7

3. Lance then copied and pasted the feathered circle selection into the grass background (**FIGURE 5:7**). Because he had feathered the selection, the edge of the portrait was softened when he pasted it into the grass window.

4. With the portrait in place, Lance opened the grayscale Buddah. Using the Pen tool he selected the Buddha, saved the resulting path, then deleted the background (**FIGURE 5:8**).

5. Lance changed the mode of the grayscale to RGB and chose Color Balance from the Adjust submenu under the Image menu. He adjusted the Buddha's grayscale to red

(**FIGURE 5:9**) and then, using the Magic Wand set at its default tolerance, he clicked once on the Buddha's darkest shadow area. He chose Similar from the Select menu to select the other shadows.

6. Before color-correcting the shadows, Lance feathered the selection by entering a Feather Radius of 4 in the Feather dialog box (**FIGURE 5:10**). He then used Color Balance to adjust the shadows to a bluish cast (**FIGURE 5:11**).

7. After color-correcting the Buddha, Lance pasted, resized, and positioned it on the grass background (**FIGURE 5:12**).

FIGURE 5:8

FIGURE 5:9

FIGURE 5:10

FIGURE 5:11

FIGURE 5:12

REVERTING PART OF AN IMAGE

Lance next cut and pasted three other images—a fish, a paint brush, and an old photograph that his father had taken of him holding a tree frog (**FIGURE 5:13**). After pasting down the three new elements, Lance decided he wanted to reposition the tree frog, which was a problem because it had been pasted down and moving it would create a hole filled with the current background color. It is possible to revert specific sections of an image to the last-saved version using the Rubber Stamp tool. Double-clicking on the Rubber Stamp icon in the tool box opens the Rubber Stamp Options dialog box, which allows you to choose the option From Saved (**FIGURE 5:14**). With From Saved selected, you can use the Rubber Stamp as you would any of the painting tools to revert sections of an image completely or gradually by changing the Opacity setting.

FIGURE 5:13

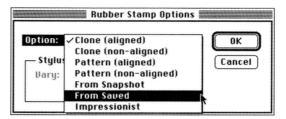

FIGURE 5:14

 If the mode or pixel dimensions of the image have been changed since the last save, the Rubber Stamp cannot be used to revert an image.

If you want to revert part of an image using the Rubber Stamp tool, you can revert only to the last version saved. This limits how often you can save, which can be risky. Lance had saved the montage each time he pasted an element, and because he had pasted the hand and tree frog before the brush and fish, he could no longer revert that area of the montage to the original grass background. He had, however, saved a version of the background without any of the elements pasted (see FIGURE 5:3), which allowed him to revert any part of the montage using the Calculate menu. To remove the hand and tree frog:

1. Lance opened the first version of the background that he had saved, and the most recent version of the montage.

The Calculate menu will work only if the images have the same pixel dimensions. If you want to revert parts of an image using this method, it is important not to change the pixel dimensions of your art as you work.

2. Using the Rectangular selection tool, Lance selected an area of the montage that included only the hand and frog. He then chose Duplicate from the Calculate submenu under the Image menu and made the Source the montage, the Source's Channel a Selection, the Destination the original grass background file, and the Destination's Channel a Selection (**FIGURE 5:15**).

3. When Lance clicked OK, a rectangular selection marquee appeared in the grass background that duplicated the selection he had made in the montage. He then copied the selected part of the grass background and pasted it into the

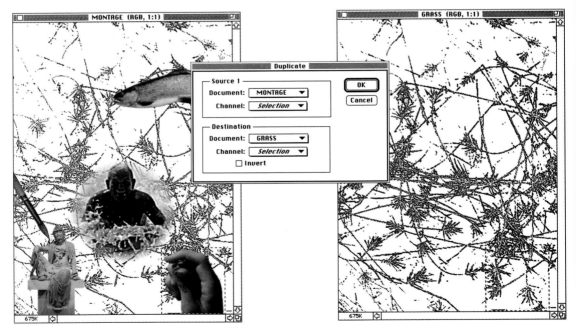

FIGURE 5:15

montage. Because the original selection was still active, the copied part of the grass background pasted into the montage in perfect register (**FIGURE 5:16**). Lance was then able to paste the hand back into the montage in a more desirable position (**FIGURE 5:17**).

Another method that works well in this situation is to make a copy of the original background by choosing All from the Select menu (Command+A) then, after selecting the part of the montage that you want to revert, choose Paste Into from the Edit menu. Again, the images must have the same pixel dimensions for this to work. This method is faster for small images where it will not take long to copy and paste the entire image. The Calculate method is best for larger images because you will copy only a small part of the image.

FIGURE 5:16

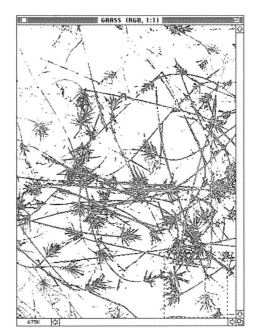

FIGURE 5:17

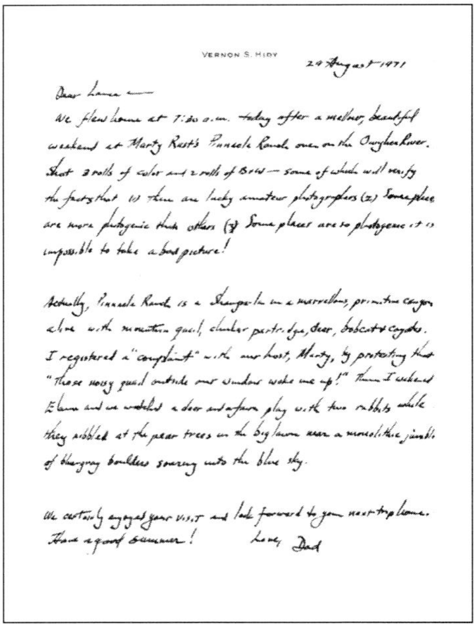

FIGURE 5:18

PASTE INTO

After repositioning the hand and frog, Lance scanned a letter that his father had written in the early seventies (**FIGURE 5:18**) and used the following procedure to add the letter to the montage.

1. Using Levels, he adjusted the gray values of the letter until its background was pure white.

2. With the Magic Wand set at a Tolerance of 0, he clicked once on the white background and then chose Similar from the Select menu to select all of the letter's white background. He then inverted the selection by choosing Inverse from the Select menu, which selected the lettering. He made a copy of the selected letters.

FIGURE 5:19

FIGURE 5:20

3. He then clicked on a white area of the montage and again chose Similar from the Select menu to select the montage's white background.

4. Finally, he chose Paste Into from the Edit menu, which pasted the letter behind the existing montage (**FIGURE 5:19**).

The final element that Lance added to the montage was a photograph that his father had taken of his mother (**FIGURE 5:20**). He silhouetted his mother's figure and her shadow, and pasted them into the montage in two stages. This allowed him to control the transparency of the shadow against the grass background, and at the same time keep the figure opaque. To finish the montage:

1. Lance used the Pen tool to select the figure and shadow as one piece. He made the resulting path into a selection by choosing Make Selection from the Paths palette. He then cut and pasted the selection into the montage.

2. After resizing and positioning the figure and shadow, he clicked once on the Type tool, and, holding down the Command key, he accessed a special Lasso tool. With the Command key pressed, he drew a selection marquee around the figure—but not the shadow. With this special Lasso tool, any floating selection that is surrounded is pasted, rather than deleted as is normally the case (**FIGURE 5:21**).

3. Lance then chose a pale gray-blue as the foreground color and pressed Option+ Delete, filling the shadow with the foreground color (**FIGURE 5:22**).

4. Finally, Lance clicked once on a selection tool, then set the Opacity in the Brushes palette to 65%, which made the shadow transparent (**FIGURE 5:23**).

FIGURE 5:21

FIGURE 5:22

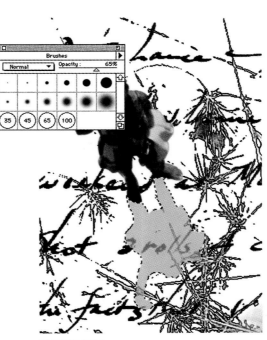

FIGURE 5:23

This piece is in honor of my father, Vernon S. "Pete" Hidy, a well-known author of books on flyfishing, who died ten years ago. He was an amateur painter, photographer, and calligrapher—interests that led to my choice of a career in the graphic arts.

—LANCE HIDY

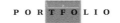

Child/Woman, Judy Dater ©1991

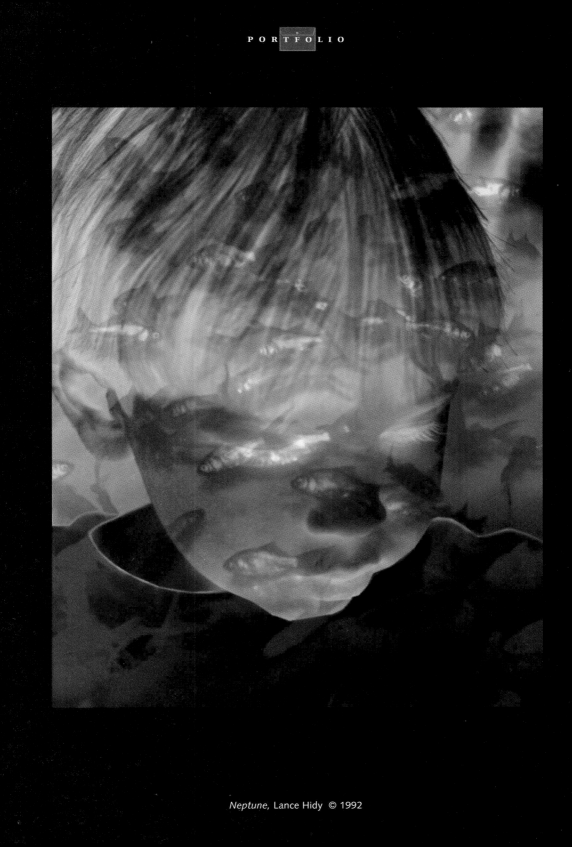

Neptune, Lance Hidy © 1992

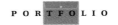

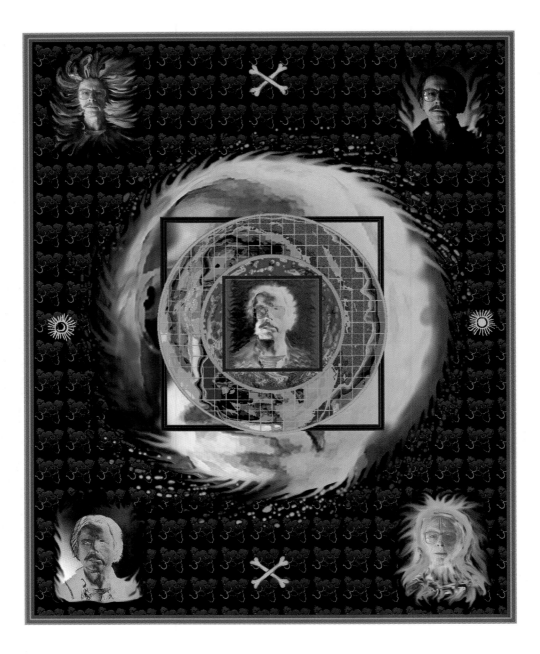

Spirit, Carl Sesto

6
MIXED MEDIA

ETIENNE DELESSERT IS A
world renowned editorial and
children's book illustrator. His
work can often be seen in the
New York Times, as well as the
Atlantic Monthly and other
magazines. More recently,
Stewart, Tabori & Chang published an extensive mono-
graph of his work. His work
has hung in galleries throughout the world, including a
one-man show at the Louvre's
Museum of Decorative Arts. In
the fall of 1992 there was a ret-
rospective of Etienne's work
in Lausanne, Switzerland,
where he was born.

Before I packed up my computer, Etienne decided to try some free-form painting without the benefit of any scans. He opened a new 700 x 730 pixel window (1.5 MB) and using only the Pencil, Brush, and Smudge tools, he produced the painting shown in **FIGURE 6:30**. After our session, we produced a print of the painting from an Iris inkjet printer. The Iris printer is capable of printing onto almost any art paper, so it is ideal for printing computer-generated limited editions.

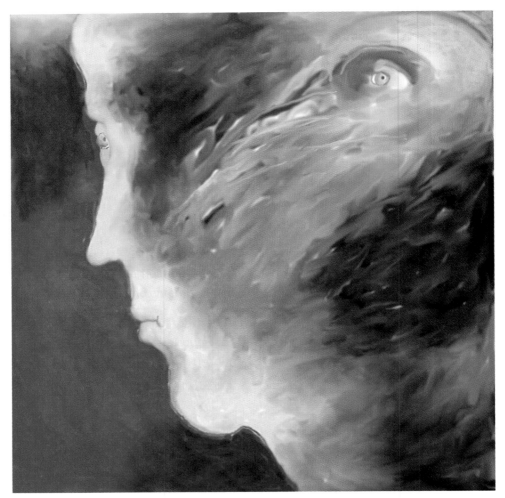

FIGURE 6:30   Etienne Delessert ©1992

Adam and Eve, Caty Bartholomew ©1992

Over the Guadalupe, Barbara Kasten ©1992 Courtesy: San Jose Hilton and Towers, Digital photo painting on canvas 25' x 7.5'

Crag Dance, Sumner Stone ©1991 Stone Type Foundry Inc.

7

OUTPUT

The artwork on this page and the following spread were created using Photoshop and Kodak's DCS-200 camera, a filmless digital camera.

As I write this book, a number of software and hardware companies are working on solutions to the problem of making color device-independent. Device independence means that your file will output with similar color on any device, whether it is an inexpensive, low-resolution inkjet printer, or a high-resolution imagesetter. The goal is to characterize every output device, input device, and display using a universal color standard so that color is predictable. Whether these solutions will be successful or an accepted standard will emerge remains to be seen.

Because of the subjective nature of color perception and the effect of ambient light on the way we perceive color—both on the printed page and on a computer's display—users are likely to have some calibration responsibilities if they desire accurate color output.

Photoshop provides a number of tools internally for calibrating a display to an output device. Unfortunately, these tools are not very intuitive, but they do work. The calibration techniques that I describe below have worked well for me, and do not require the expense of extra software or hardware. This method is based on each user's color perception, rather than any mechanical means. Whether you use these techniques or invest in another hardware or software solution, you cannot expect to match output to your display without first calibrating to the output device.

COLOR MODELS

The first calibration step is to have a basic understanding of the two color models used in electronic publishing—RGB and CMYK. Your RGB monitor may be capable of displaying 16 million colors, but not all RGB colors can be printed using CMYK ink. The monitor's RGB color has a much larger gamut than the CMYK inks used by printers (gamut is a color model's entire range of color). The limited nature of process ink is nothing new; color separators have always had to sacrifice matching certain colors for the economy of the CMYK system. If you are familiar with the gamuts of both the RGB and CMYK color models, you will have a better chance of matching printed output to your display.

RGB COLOR   The color displayed on your monitor is called *additive color* (see **FIGURE 7:1,** *RGB and CMYK Color*). Red, green, and blue are the primary additive colors; by adding varying combinations and intensities of these three colors, a

RGB and CMYK Color

Light is made up of varying wavelengths, which we perceive as color depending on the wavelength's frequency. Red has the longest visible wavelength and violet the shortest. White light can be divided into three primary colors—red, green, and blue. A monitor's display is divided into small cells containing red, green, and blue phosphors that, when stimulated with electricity, emit combinations of red, green, and blue light. When your monitor adds the RGB colors together at full intensity, the result is white on your display (FIGURE A). If only two of the RGB colors are combined at full intensity, a new color is created. FIGURE B shows how adding only the red and green parts of the spectrum at full intensity results in yellow. By adding different combinations and intensities of the RGB colors, your monitor is capable of displaying a wide range of color.

CMYK ink on paper works in a very different way than your monitor's RGB phosphors. Depending on the pigment's color, the ink absorbs or reflects parts of the visible spectrum. Yellow ink absorbs (subtracts) the blue part of the spectrum and then reflects red and green light back to our eyes, which we perceive as yellow (FIGURE C).

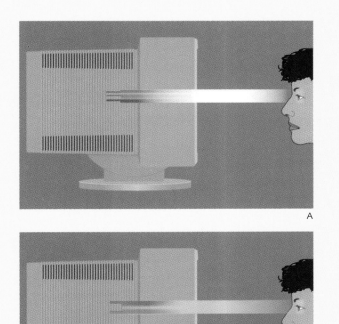

A

B

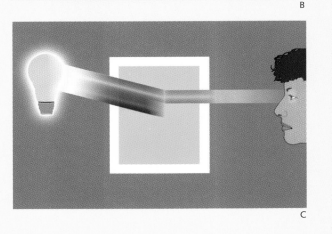

C

large gamut of colors can be produced. Adding red, green, and blue at full intensity results in white on your display. The RGB monitor's gamut is very large, but it cannot come close to displaying the entire visible spectrum. There are even some CMYK colors that cannot be displayed accurately on an RGB monitor (most notably 100 percent cyan), even though the CMYK gamut is much narrower than the RGB gamut (**FIGURE 7:2**).

Since the RGB gamut is larger than the CMYK gamut, there are many displayed colors that cannot be printed by four-color process. This difference in gamuts presents the first calibration problem. If you expect to match output to your display, you cannot use the out-of-gamut colors in the RGB model. Photoshop addresses this problem in two ways. When you select color with Photoshop's Color Picker, occasionally an exclamation point with a small color patch beneath it appears next to the newly selected color in the Color Picker's dialog box. The exclamation point indicates that the selected color is not printable with CMYK ink; the patch indicates the closest printable

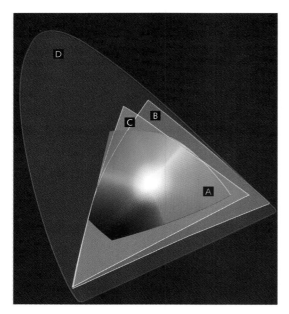

All input, output, and display devices have a color gamut, or range of possible color, that is a subset of the entire visible spectrum. CMYK color (A) has a very narrow range of color relative to all visible color (D). Photographic film (B) and an RGB monitor (C) have a larger gamut of color, but their gamuts are still much narrower than visible color. Because the entire gamuts of visible color, monitor color, and film color cannot be printed, the unprintable parts of their gamuts are represented here as gray.

FIGURE 7:2

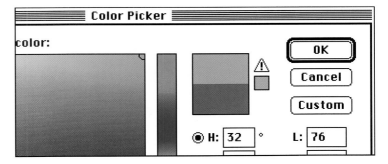

FIGURE 7:3

color (**FIGURE 7:3**). Clicking on the exclamation point replaces the current out-of-gamut color with the closest printable color. The exclamation point also appears in the floating Info palette accessed under the Window menu.

 The way Photoshop converts out-of-gamut colors into CMYK colors is much more accurate with version 2.5. If you are using version 2.0 and you choose an out-of-gamut blue, the color Photoshop 2.0 uses to replace the blue is often violet. This undesirable shift in hue rather than saturation has been fixed with 2.5.

The other way to ensure that out-of-gamut colors are not used is to work in the CMYK mode. In this case, the color palette from which you can choose is limited to the CMYK gamut. If you work in RGB mode and convert to CMYK mode, any unprintable colors are replaced with printable ones when you make the conversion.

CMYK COLOR   The color model of the printing press is CMYK color. CMYK is called *subtractive* color (**FIGURE 7:1C**). Ink on a printed page absorbs or reflects different wavelengths (colors) of light depending on the pigment. The wavelengths that are reflected back to your eye are perceived as different colors. When the three subtractive primaries (CMY) are combined at 100 percent, the result is close to black (**FIGURE 7:4**). This is because most of the visible colors in the spectrum are being subtracted by the pigment, while very little is reflected. Because of the impurities in the pigments of CMY printing inks, a perfect black cannot be made when cyan, magenta, and yellow are combined; therefore black must be added as a fourth color.

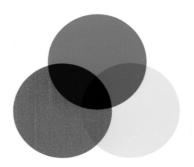

FIGURE 7:4

 CMYK printing is generally referred to as subtractive color, but strictly speaking it is a complex mix of both additive and subtractive color. For example, when 50 percent magenta and 50 percent yellow halftone dots are mixed, they appear orange. The two pigments absorb some light and reflect the rest. Because the dots are small we do not perceive them individually as magenta and yellow, but as an additive combination of the two—orange.

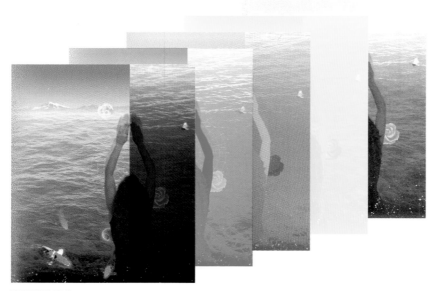

FIGURE 7:5

Photoshop allows you to edit images in either CMYK or RGB mode. When you work in CMYK mode, you are given an RGB color preview to work with, and as you work, the four CMYK channels are edited. This means that it is not necessary to convert from RGB to CMYK when you have the file output (**FIGURE 7:5**). However, CMYK files contain a fourth channel, so they are larger than RGB files; when converted to CMYK, a 10 MB RGB file becomes 13.3 MB. The preview of a CMYK file also refreshes on the screen at a noticeably slower rate, although the refresh rate for both RGB and CMYK modes has been improved with version 2.5. Usually the benefits of working in CMYK mode are not worth the slowdown in performance, so I generally work in RGB mode.

There are some situations that warrant working in CMYK mode. High-end scanners often make conversions from RGB to CMYK that are superior to those done by Photoshop (see Chapter One, *Comparing Scanners*). When you buy a CMYK scan from a service bureau or trade shop, you should work in CMYK mode, particularly if you are keeping the color reasonably close to the color of the original. If, on the other hand, you are changing color radically, chances are you will lose the high-end scanner's conversion benefits. In this case RGB is faster and, as described below, working in RGB mode and then making the conversion to CMYK with Photoshop gives you more control calibrating to different output devices.

ADJUSTING OUT-OF-GAMUT COLORS   If you decide to work in RGB mode and you are not familiar with the restrictions of the CMYK gamut, I recommend converting to CMYK in order to preview any color shifts. You may be dissatisfied with the way Photoshop makes this conversion. If that is the case, you can bring out-of-gamut RGB colors into the CMYK gamut manually before you convert to CMYK. To do this, open the Info palette and then choose Hue/Saturation from the Adjust

Color changes appearance depending on the temperature of the ambient light. Fluorescent light can make a color seem bluer, while incandescent light can make the same color appear yellower.

menu. When the cursor is moved onto the image, it changes to an Eyedropper cursor. The Info palette shows two sets of values—the values to the left represent the original pixel values read from the eyedropper, and the values on the right change to reflect your adjustments. You can then adjust the Saturation and Lightness until the exclamation points disappear, indicating that the color is now printable.

CALIBRATION

The differences in RGB and CMYK color and the generally subjective nature of color perception make matching an RGB display to CMYK printing somewhat difficult. Perfect matches are almost impossible. However, the difficulties of matching the output to the display have more to do with the nature of color perception and the limitations of CMYK color than with deficiencies in RGB display. Color on both the display and the printed page can change depending on the ambient light—a printed red will change appearance depending on whether it is viewed under incandescent or fluorescent light (**FIGURE 7:6**). The color gamut of photography and artwork is much larger than that of printed CMYK and, because of this limitation, traditional color separators have never been able to perfectly match CMYK color to photographic color either.

While perfect color matches between the RGB monitor and CMYK printing are difficult to achieve, they can be very close. Below is an explanation of the calibration techniques I use. Calibration is a three-part process:

- Stabilize your viewing conditions.
- Adjust your monitor to display color the same way over time.
- Create and save Printing Inks Setup preferences files for each output device you send to.

Accurate calibration takes some time and effort on your part, but if you do not calibrate and create separation preferences for each output device you send files to, it is unlikely that the resulting output will be acceptable.

STABLE VIEWING CONDITIONS   The output from a professionally run service bureau or trade shop always remains consistent—if you send the same file to the same output device more than once, the output should look the same each time the file is run. An imagesetter needs constant attention to maintain consistent output, and this consistency is critical if you are to have any chance of matching output to your display. An imagesetter that does not output consistently is a moving target, which will make the task of calibrating to it impossible. You should find a service bureau that constantly monitors and calibrates their output devices.

If you are sure that the output is consistent, then the next step in the calibration process is to make sure your monitor displays color consistently. If both your display and the various output devices that you send your file to are stable, then a file can be separated from RGB to CMYK in different ways to account for variations in each device's output.

To ensure that your monitor's display is consistent:

1. The ideal working environment is a windowless room, with neutral gray walls and lighting that never changes. Shifting ambient light has a subtle but noticeable effect on your display's color.

2. If you work in a room with windows, cover the windows with shades.

3. Avoid completely darkened or brightly lit rooms. The ideal lighting is to eliminate any overhead light and then view reflective art from a 5,000° K light box positioned behind the monitor (FIGURE 7:7). Sylvania makes a fluorescent bulb called Design 50 that is rated at 5,000° K.

4. Set your monitor's brightness control knob at about the halfway mark, and then tape it down so that it is not accidentally changed from one working session to the next.

5. Make sure your monitor has warmed up for at least twenty minutes before making any critical color corrections.

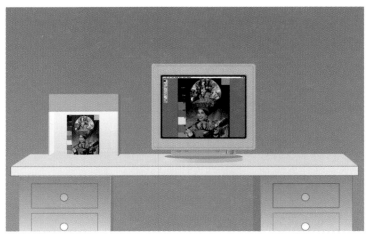

The ideal working conditions are a windowless room with no overhead lighting to reflect off the monitor. A 5000° K light box behind the display is ideal for comparing printed art to the displayed art. Good viewing conditions are essential for matching output to your monitor.

FIGURE 7:7

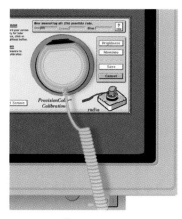

FIGURE 7:8

Hardware calibrators adjust a monitor's display to be consistent over time. They do not, however, guarantee that the printed art will match the displayed art.

GAMMA AND COLOR TEMPERATURE You may have noticed that the televisions in a retail showroom all display color in a slightly different way; they vary in saturation and warmth or coolness of color. Computer displays have a similar problem. A file will rarely look exactly the same on different monitors, even if the monitors are manufactured by the same company. Most uncalibrated monitors have a distinct bluish cast when they are shipped, which is not acceptable if you are preparing art for print.

A number of monitor manufacturers make hardware calibrators that allow you to change the *gamma* and *color temperature* of a monitor. The calibrator allows you to set your monitor to a standard that can be duplicated over time, adjusting for factors such as heat and humidity and the monitor's age. The device is usually a sensor that attaches to the face of your display with a suction cup; the sensor reads a test pattern of the monitor's red, green, and blue values, and adjusts the display for any deficiencies (**FIGURE 7:8**). If you use a hardware calibrator, you should calibrate your display about once a month. It is important to understand that calibrators do not guarantee a color match to any specific output device; their only purpose is to stabilize your display. Calibration to a specific device is done via Photoshop's Printing Inks and Monitors preferences files.

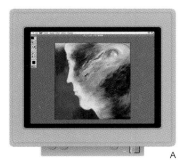

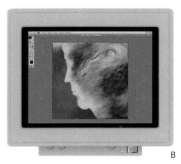

Figure A shows a monitor set at 5,000° K, which is an appropriate setting for print-related use. Figure B shows an uncalibrated monitor with a blue cast that resembles 15 percent cyan.

A   B

FIGURE 7:9

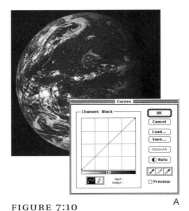 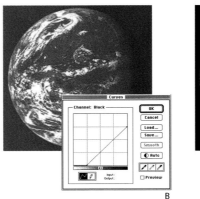 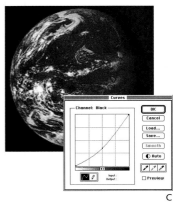

FIGURE 7:10   A   B   C

Figure B shows how an image becomes less contrasted when its values are lightened uniformly (by 10 percent in this case). If the values are adjusted on a curve where the middle values are adjusted more than the highlights and shadows (C), the result accurately relects the way we see. The curve is called gamma.

Color temperature is the perceived warmth or coolness of white on your display measured in degrees Kelvin. White on an uncalibrated display has cool blue cast that resembles 10 percent to 15 percent cyan, which is very difficult to compensate for in your output. Adjusting the monitor's temperature to between 5,000° K and 5,500° K displays white as the approximate color of white paper viewed in daylight, and is an ideal setting for print-related output (**FIGURE 7:9**). If you plan to print on paper that is not pure white, you should adjust your monitor's white point to match the paper.

Gamma is the lightness or darkness of your display, adjusted for the way we perceive values. Computers display the gray scale in an evenly distributed way, while our eyes compress the dark and light ends of the gray scale so that we see images in higher contrast. Adjusting the gamma is a way to alter a monitor's middle tones relative to the way we see (**FIGURE 7:10**). I set my monitor to a gamma of 2.0 (**FIGURE 7:11**).

If you cannot justify the added expense of a hardware calibrator, Adobe provides a software calibrator when you purchase Photoshop. On the disk labeled *Calibration disk,* there is a control panel device named Gamma. Make sure that you put Gamma into your system folder so that it shows up in your control panel. Gamma is very easy and intuitive to use (see your *Photoshop User Guide* for detailed instructions). It allows you to change the gamma and color balance of your display interactively (**FIGURE 7:12**). The disadvantage of Gamma is that it cannot adjust for slight changes that might occur due to aging of the monitor or surrounding heat and humidity. Once you have settled on the gamma and color temperature for your display, you should not change them, so that what you see on screen will be consistent from one working session to the next.

CALIBRATING TO AN OUTPUT DEVICE

With your viewing conditions stabilized, you can now calibrate to a specific output device. It is likely that you will have Photoshop art output on several devices. You might proof the file on a color printer before going to the expense of having separations made, or you may use different vendors for high-resolution output. A well-maintained output device outputs the same file consistently time after time; but it is unlikely that the same file output from both an inkjet printer and imagesetter, or, for that matter, from two imagesetters, will match. This poses an obvious problem—what good is an inexpensive proof if it does not come close to predicting the color of final film separations?

Photoshop allows you to adjust how an image is converted from RGB to CMYK and, in the process, to account for the inconsistencies between output devices. These adjustments are made, depending on the information you enter, in the Monitors Setup and Printing Inks Setup dialog boxes in the Preferences submenu under File. You can then save the preferences files you create for each output device and load them before converting from RGB to CMYK.

Figure A shows a calibrated display set at 5000° K and 1.2 gamma. Figure B shows a calibrated display set at 5000° K and 2.0 gamma.

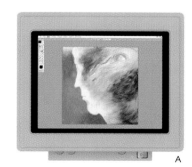
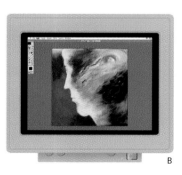

A   B

FIGURE 7:11

Below is the procedure for calibrating and creating prefer-ences files for a specific output device. You should have to do this only once for each device that you output from, unless of course the service bureau changes the color characteristics of their proofing system, or your lighting conditions change, in which case you would have to recalibrate.

FIGURE 7:12

OLÉ NO MOIRE   The first step in calibrating to a specific output device is to have your service bureau run a test proof from the device to which you want to calibrate. The *Photoshop User Guide* suggests calibrating to a press proof. A press proof is a proof made from the film separations on a printing press that allows you to account and adjust for the many variables that occur in the printing process after the film is made. This of course assumes a rather large printing budget, which most users do not have. I will assume here that you will be matching to a laminated color proof made directly from the film. These proofs accurately predict the color on press much less expen-sively than a press proof does; Match Print, Chromalin, Fu-jiprint, and Agfaproof are common proofing systems.

Adobe provides an excellent CMYK test file for calibration, named Olé No Moiré, found on the Photoshop disk labeled *Calibration disk.* If you are using version 2.5, launch the Photo-shop Installer and install the calibration folder. This file is par-ticularly useful for calibrating because the image has a wide range of color and gray values along with 100 percent CMYK color patches. Many service bureaus will output Olé No Moiré at no charge (**FIGURE 7:13**).

If you use Olé No Moiré for a calibration test, make sure the service bureau has not altered the file in any way. If there is a question, have the CMYK file, from which the color proof was made, sent along with the test proof. If you are sure that the test print was printed from an unalt-ered Olé No Moiré file, you can use the file provided on your Photoshop Calibration disk for calibrating.

FIGURE 7:13

ADJUSTING THE CMYK PREVIEW You can adjust the lightness and darkness and, in a limited way, the color of a CMYK file's preview using the Printing Inks Setup and Monitors Setup dialog boxes located in the Preferences submenu under the File menu. The adjustments you make with these preference files affect *only* the preview and not the underlying CMYK values. This is different from the adjustment and color correction tools in the Adjust submenu, which change both the preview *and* the CMYK percentages. Matching the CMYK preview to a color proof using the preference files calibrates your monitor to the devices that made the film and proof. Remember, you should repeat this process for each device you send to. After calibrating, you can then save the preferences and load them, depending on the device for which you are preparing the file.

 The preview of an RGB file is not affected in any way by Printing Inks or Monitors preferences. The file must be in CMYK mode for these preferences to affect the preview.

Use the following procedure for calibrating to a specific device:

1. Open the CMYK Olé No Moiré file. If you make your own test file you must have the unaltered CMYK file that generated the test print for the calibration to work properly.

2. Choose Monitor Setup from the Preferences submenu. Under Gamma, enter the gamma to which you have set your monitor. If you are using a hardware calibrator, enter the temperature to which you have set your monitor in the White Point pop-up menu (if you are using Photoshop's Gamma software, leave the White Point at the default 6,500°K). Choose your monitor's model from the Phosphor Colors menu, and choose Medium from the Ambient Light menu (**FIGURE 7:14**).

FIGURE 7:14

3. Compare the preview on the screen to the color proof. It is not likely that the preview and the proof match, but if they do, skip step 4. If the proof does not match the screen—for example, if it is too dark, as in **FIGURE 7:15**—choose Printing Inks Setup from the Preferences submenu.

4. The default for Printing Inks Setup is SWOP (coated) with 20% Dot Gain. If you increase the Dot Gain percentage and click OK, the values of the on-screen preview will darken; adjust the Dot Gain until the proof and preview match in value (**FIGURE 7:16**). Leave Use Dot Gain for Grayscale Images unchecked.

If you can match the proof by simply adjusting the Dot Gain percentage, you are finished

calibrating to the device that output the proof. It is likely though that there may also be a shift in color for which you want to compensate; for example, the proof may seem to have too much red compared to the screen, as shown in **FIGURE 7:17**. To compensate for color shifts:

1. Open Levels (Command+L) and, using *only* the middle Input slider, adjust the individual CMYK channels until the display matches the proof. You can adjust each CMYK channel separately by clicking the radio buttons labeled C, M, Y, and K at the bottom of the dialog box. Do not use the Master button in this process, and make sure that Preview is checked. When you move the middle slider, the middle number to the right of Input Levels changes

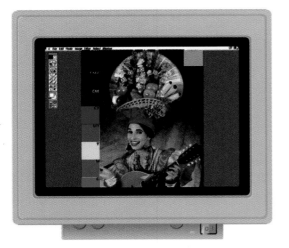

FIGURE 7:15

FIGURE 7:16

FIGURE 7:17

accordingly (**FIGURE 7:18**). When the preview matches the proof, write down the middle number for each channel that you have adjusted and click Cancel. *Make sure that you do not click* OK.

2. Open Printing Inks Setup and choose Custom from the Ink Colors pop-up menu (if Custom is already chosen, click on it). A menu appears that shows the different combinations of CMYK colors at 100 percent (**FIGURE 7:19**). To the right of the color patches are four boxes that allow you to adjust the gray balance. If you are using version 2.5, the Gray Balance boxes are at the first level of the Printing Inks Setup dialog box. Enter the numbers that you noted from the Levels dialog box in the corresponding Gray Balance boxes labeled C, M, Y, and K. The default is 1.00 for each color, which corresponds to the 1.00 default of the middle Input slider in Levels. Click OK to return to Printing Inks Setup, and click OK again. The new preview should now match the proof (**FIGURE 7:20**).

With some experience, you can skip the step of using Levels to find the Gray Balance numbers—for example, lowering the number in the M box, under Gray Balance, increases

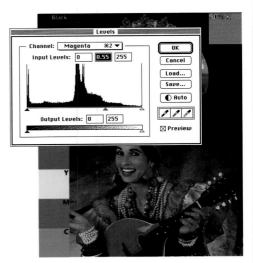

FIGURE 7:18

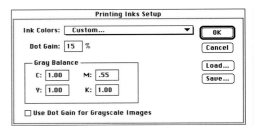

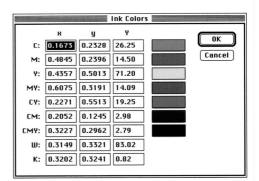

FIGURE 7:19

FIGURE 7:20

the amount of magenta in the image's preview, raising the number decreases the magenta, and so on.

 If you decide to return to Levels to read- just for a color shift, make sure that you first reset the Gray Balance settings to the default 1.00 for each of the C, M, Y, and K boxes, then repeat the process.

Because of the differences in RGB and CMYK color, it is impossible to exactly match all of the color patches on the Olé No Moiré proof (you will not be able to perfectly match the cyan patch, but you can get close). The set of CMYK patches in the Ink Colors dialog box correspond to the CMYK patches on Olé No

Moiré. You can adjust the color of these patches to more closely resemble the Olé No Moiré patches. Click on any of the patches and a Color Picker appears that allows you to make adjustments to that color. The *Photoshop User Guide* suggests that you do not change these colors, but I have found that they are usually quite far off, particularly for low-end color printers.

It is easier to calibrate to an imagesettter than to some color printers. Color printers all have slightly different gamuts, which can be difficult to account for. Also, some printers have difficulty rendering the highlights of an image accurately.

SAVING CALIBRATION PREFERENCES

Photoshop uses the information that you enter in the Printing Inks Setup and Monitor Setup preferences to adjust the way an RGB to CMYK conversion is made. If you have darkened the on-screen image to match a test print that is too dark, then Photoshop uses that preference to make a CMYK conversion that is appropriately lighter without changing the RGB preview. The output of a CMYK file separated with this preference will be lighter and will match the preview.

You can view the CMYK channels individually by choosing Cyan, Magenta, Yellow, or Black from the Channels palette. If you separate the same RGB file twice using different preference settings, and then open both files and compare their channels, the channels look different but their previews look the same (**FIGURE 7:21**). Conversely, if you load different Monitor Setup and Printing Inks Setup preferences while previewing the same CMYK file, the preview will change, while the channels remain the same; this allows you to preview how one CMYK file would output from different devices (**FIGURE 7:22**).

It is likely you will use different output devices to generate color proofs and film separations. Of course, you do not want to constantly recalibrate, so you should save the Printing Inks Setup preferences that you created for each output device. You can then load the saved settings before making a separation for a specific device. To save different Printing Inks Setup preferences:

1. Create a folder on your hard disk and name it Printing Inks Prefs.

2. After you have matched the CMYK preview to the test print, open Printing Inks Setup and click on Save. A dialog box

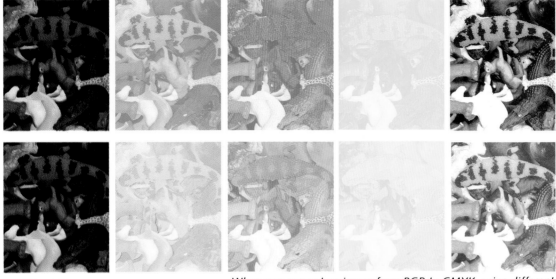

FIGURE 7:21

When you convert an image from RGB to CMYK, using different Printing Ink, Monitor, or Separation Setup preference settings, its preview remains the same, but its underlying CMYK values change.

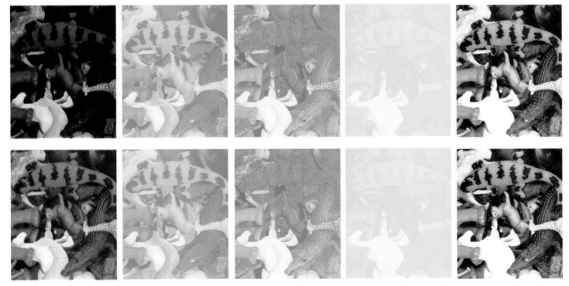

FIGURE 7:22

When you load different Printing Ink, Monitor, or Separation Setup preference settings while an image is in CMYK mode, its preview will change, while its underlying CMYK values remain the same.

appears that allows you to name and save the current settings. Name the file after the output device to which you have just calibrated.

3. Locate the Printing Inks Prefs folder that you saved on your hard disk and click Save.

4. *Before* you convert an RGB file to CMYK, you must first load the appropriate Printing Inks Setup preferences for the device from which the file is to be output. If you want to output the file from two different devices, you must make two RGB-to-CMYK conversions with the correct Printing Inks Setup preferences loaded.

5. To load a saved Printing Inks Setup preference file, open Printing Inks Setup, click on Load, and find the Printing Inks Prefs folder on your hard disk. Locate the file you saved for the device from which you will output the file, and double-click on it. Click OK.

Always leave your Monitor Setup preferences the same, because they also affect the RGB to CMYK conversions. If you want to change both the Monitor Setup and Printing Inks Setup for a specific device, you should save them as a separation table (see Saving a Separation Table *later in this chapter).*

Once you have calibrated and saved Printing Inks Setup preferences for each output device that you use, save a master RGB file and then separate it differently depending on the device to which it is sent. If you need to make adjustments to a file after it has been output, edit the master RGB file and then re-separate it using the appropriate Printing Inks Setup, rather than editing one of the CMYK versions.

FIGURE 7:23

CALIBRATING FOR GRAYSCALE IMAGES

Photoshop 2.5 allows you to calibrate for grayscale printing, which was not easily accomplished with earlier versions. You can now allow the dot gain that you set in Printing Inks Setup to affect the preview of a grayscale image. To calibrate for grayscales:

1. Make a test file of a grayscale image that includes a full range of grays. You might want to include a grayscale bar, which you can make by selecting a rectangle and filling it with a blend from white to black (**FIGURE 7:23**).

2. If you can afford it, output the test file as a film negative from the imagesetter that you will be using, and have your printer run a press proof from the negative. If you cannot afford a press proof, have a black-only color proof made. This will predict

some dot gain that might occur on press. You could also have a contact print made of the negative, but this will not predict any dot gain.

3. Preview the test file on your monitor. Choose Printing Inks Setup from the Preferences submenu, check Use Dot Gain for Grayscale Images, and click OK. Compare the test file to the test print. If the preview is too light or dark, increase or decrease the Dot Gain setting in the Printing Inks Setup to adjust it (**FIGURE 7:24**).

4. When you have matched the preview (**FIGURE 7:25**), save the new Printing Inks Setup by clicking save. Name the file and save it in your Printing Inks Prefs folder.

5. Load the saved Printing Inks Setup preferences for the printer you will be using before you edit your grayscale scans.

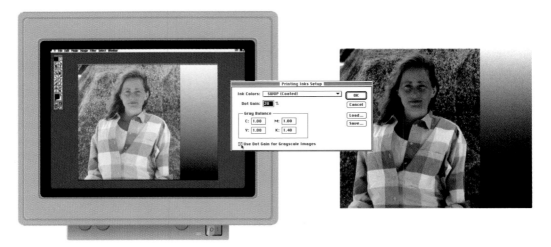

FIGURE 7:24

Be aware that if Use Dot Gain for Grayscale Images is checked in the Printing Inks Setup dialog box, it affects the preview of grayscale images without affecting the data. Do not edit grayscale images without first loading the proper Printing Inks Setup.

SEPARATION SETUP

When you make a CMYK separation, there is a third set of preferences that affect the way the conversion is made. The Separation Setup preferences determine how the black plate is created. Converting from RGB to CMY is a relatively simple process, but generating the black plate is more problematic since it must be interpolated. The information that you enter in the Separation Setup dialog box determines

how the black separation is made. The default Separation Setup settings generally produce acceptable results, so unless you have experience making four-color separations, you should use the default settings. Below is an overview of the Separation Setup dialog box; with it I will give some very general guidelines for various settings.

The Separation Setup preferences have no affect on either an RGB or CMYK preview. They do affect the underlying CMYK percentages when you make a separation. If you change any of the Separation Setup settings, you must reseparate the original RGB file for them to take effect.

GCR AND UCR Gray Component Replacement (GCR) and Under Color Removal (UCR) are two separation strategies that replace

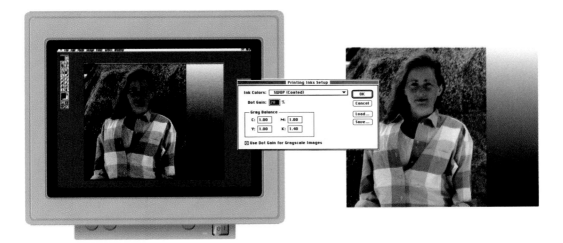

FIGURE 7:25

some of the CMY color with black. This makes the color on press more predictable and manageable, and it can also save ink costs (black is the least expensive of the four inks, which can be significant in long runs). GCR is Photoshop's default; it employs a method by which the color that adds definition and shape to the image is replaced with black. For instance, if a fleshtone is made primarily with magenta and yellow and its shadows are defined with cyan, some of the cyan is replaced with black. This theoretically makes the fleshtone less susceptible to unwanted color shifts on press.

UCR removes gray colors made with all three CMY colors and replaces them with an appropriate percentage of black ink. GCR is the method many separators prefer because it allows more control in making the black plate. Ask your printer which method he or she prefers.

BLACK GENERATION   Black Generation dictates how much density there is in the black plate when you make a GCR separation. There are five options available: None (makes a CMY-only separation), Light, Medium, Heavy, and Maximum. The default is Medium. **FIGURE 7:26** shows how different black generations affect an image.

INK LIMITS   You can limit the overall density of the ink coverage and the maximum density of the black ink by adjusting the Total Ink Limit and Black Ink Limit percentages. The default setting for Total Ink Limit is 300%; this means that the maximum combined percentages of the four inks will never exceed 300 percent in any given part of the image. When the total ink density exceeds 300 percent on a four-color press, the ink

You can affect how the black plate is created, when GCR is choosen as the separation method, by altering the Black Generation setting. Neutral colored images are most noticeably affected by black generation. Here I have separated the same image five times using different black generation settings.

FIGURE 7:26   *None*   *Light*

Images with deep shadow areas can benefit from Under Color Addition. UCA adds color back into the separation, that would be removed via GCR, resulting in richer shadow areas. Here I have separated the same image five times using different UCA settings.

FIGURE 7:27   *0%*   *25%*

Medium   *Heavy*   *Maximum*

50%   *75%*   *100%*

might not dry properly and there is the risk that the ink will offset onto another sheet.

The Black Ink Limit allows you to adjust the maximum percentage of black ink that is generated. The default setting is 100%. I like to lower this percentage to about 95% so that the shadow areas do not fill in.

UCA AMOUNT   Under Color Addition (UCA) allows you to add color back in that has been removed via the GCR process. The default setting is 0%. If your separations are printing flat in the shadow areas, adding some color back in (20 percent to 50 percent is usually adequate) can give some definition to the print. FIGURE 7:27 shows Medium Black Generation with different amounts of color added back.

TRAPPING

There are some kinds of Photoshop images that you should trap. Trapping creates a small amount of intermediate color between complementary colors, so that if the press goes off register, a white space will not show between the color. For instance, if you do not trap when bright red appears next to pure cyan, and the cyan plate shifts slightly out of regis-

ter, a white edge will show between the two colors. To prevent this from happening, the two colors must overlap. If an image has no obvious color breaks, then trapping is not necessary. Also, you should not trap low-resolution art where the pixel shows—the minimum trap size is one pixel, which would be too obtrusive in a low-resolution file.

Photoshop has a trapping option that is very simple to use. To trap an image, you must first convert it to CMYK mode. Choose Trap from the Image menu and a dialog box appears that allows you to choose the size of the trap in pixels, points, or millimeters. I use one pixel; if for some reason you are working with an image that is more than 400 ppi, specify two pixels. When you click OK, any adjacent areas made up of complementary colors will be given a one-pixel border that is a mix of the two colors (**FIGURE 7:28**)

Trapping in Photoshop is much easier than it is in a drawing program. If you use Adobe Illustrator, consider importing complex drawings into Photoshop for trapping and output. See Chapter Three, Importing from Illustrator, *for details on how to import Illustrator drawings.*

SAVING A SEPARATION TABLE

You may find that you are adjusting the Printing Inks and Separation Setup preferences differently for each output device that you use. If that is the case, simply saving the Printing Inks preferences will not be adequate. You can save all of the preference settings you create for each output device as a *separation table*. You then load the appropriate table before an RGB to CMYK conversion is made. Loading a separation table also saves some time because Photoshop does not have to create a new table, which takes a few minutes. Photoshop 2.5 makes it easier to create separation tables, but they are a very useful feature in both versions of the program.

To save a separation table using Photoshop 2.5:

1. After you have matched the CMYK preview to the proof using the Printing Inks Setup preferences and entered the desired Separation Setup, choose Separation Tables from the Preferences submenu.

FIGURE 7:28

1 pixel trap

FIGURE 7:29

FIGURE 7:30

2. The Separation Tables dialog box appears which allows to save the current Preference settings for Monitor, Printing Inks, and Separation Setup as one file. Click Use Separation Setup under To CMYK, and Use Printing Inks Setup under From CMYK, and then click Save (**FIGURE 7:29**). A dialog box appears, allowing you to save the table to your disk.

3. To load a saved table, choose Separation Tables and click Load. Find the desired table on your drive and click Open. When you load a table, Use Table is checked with the table's name to its right, both To CMYK and From CMYK (**FIGURE 7:30**). Do not change these settings; click OK. Now when you convert from RGB to CMYK, the loaded table overrides the current settings in Monitor, Printing Inks, and Separation Setup. If you want to use other settings, you must first either load another table or choose Separation Tables and then click Use Separation Setup and Use Printing Inks Setup.

To save a separation table using Photoshop 2.0:

1. After you have matched the CMYK preview to the proof using the Printing Inks Setup preferences and entered the desired Separation Setup, open a new RGB file (Command+N).

2. Change the mode of this new file from RGB Color to CMYK Color under the Mode menu. A box will appear that reads: *Building Color Separation Table.*

		Photoshop Plug-Ins			
40 items		63.1 MB in disk		49.4 MB available	

Name	Size	Label	Last Modified
NTSC Colors	4K	—	Fri, Jun 14, 1991, 3:47 AM
Paths to Illustrator	8K	—	Mon, Oct 7, 1991, 3:33 PM
PCX Format	12K	—	Fri, Jun 14, 1991, 3:47 AM
Pict Resource	16K	—	Fri, Jun 14, 1991, 3:47 AM
Pinch	6K	—	Fri, Jun 14, 1991, 3:47 AM
Pointillize	10K	—	Fri, Jun 14, 1991, 3:47 AM
Polar Coordinates	6K	—	Fri, Jun 14, 1991, 3:47 AM
PS Prefs	16K	—	Mon, Jan 18, 1993, 1:34 PM
PS Table	100K	—	Sun, Jan 17, 1993, 8:09 PM
Radial Blur	12K	—	Fri, Jun 14, 1991, 3:47 AM
RGBTable.TIFF	76K	—	Fri, Nov 1, 1991, 7:23 PM
Ripple	124K	—	Fri, Jun 14, 1991, 3:47 AM
ScanMaker Plug-In	278K	—	Wed, Feb 12, 1992, 10:57 AM
ScanMaker.pre	152K	—	Wed, Nov 18, 1992, 10:14 PM

FIGURE 7:31

		Photoshop Plug-Ins			
40 items		62.9 MB in disk		49.5 MB available	

Name	Size	Label	Last Modified
1 / RAW TABLE SPECS	8K	—	Sun, Oct 25, 1992, 3:21 PM
1 /CCI	100K	—	Wed, Dec 30, 1992, 1:45 PM
1 /CCI HUE	104K	—	Fri, Nov 13, 1992, 2:24 PM
1 /DONNELLEY	100K	—	Sun, Jan 17, 1993, 1:16 PM
1 /GE DEMO	100K	—	Mon, Dec 7, 1992, 8:26 AM
1 /GRAPHICS EXPRESS	100K	—	Thu, Nov 19, 1992, 12:03 PM
1 /HK	100K	—	Wed, Oct 21, 1992, 11:39 AM
1 /ILLUSTRATOR	100K	—	Wed, Oct 21, 1992, 11:41 AM
1 /RWB.	100K	—	Tue, Nov 10, 1992, 12:52 PM
Adobe JPEG	76K	—	Fri, Nov 1, 1991, 3:03 PM
Crystallize	10K	—	Fri, Jun 14, 1991, 3:47 AM
DCS-200.HEX	80K	—	Tue, Oct 20, 1992, 8:00 AM
De-Interlace	6K	—	Fri, Jun 14, 1991, 3:47 AM
Displace	10K	—	Fri, Jun 14, 1991, 3:47 AM

FIGURE 7:32

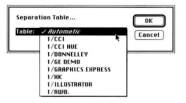

FIGURE 7:33

3. When the mode change is complete, close the new file without saving.

4. Go to the Finder (if you use System 6.08 or earlier and are not using Multifinder, quit Photoshop) and open your Photoshop Plug-ins folder, which should be located inside the Photoshop folder. Look for a file named PS Table (**FIGURE 7:31**), which contains all the preference settings based on the last RGB-TO-CMYK conversion made—in this case the conversion of the new RGB file you just opened. Rename the PS Table file to reflect the output device to which you have just calibrated. (I usually start the name with a space so that all of my tables are at the top of the folder list when viewed by name. See **FIGURE 7:32**.)

5. Return to Photoshop. Hold down the Option key and choose Separation Setup from the Preferences submenu. When you release the mouse button, a pop-up menu appears with a list of all the tables you have created (**FIGURE 7:33**). When you want to send a file to a specific output device, open the RGB file to be output, choose the table you have saved for that device, and convert to CMYK.

APPENDIX A
File Formats

Once you have finished a Photoshop illustration, you may want to export the artwork to a page layout or drawing program, where type or flat color can be added. Moving Photoshop art into other programs saves the time and cost of mechanically stripping the art and type together. Exporting also gives you the opportunity to use type and imagery in ways that would be impossible or too expensive to create traditionally. There are, however, some technical problems that come with exporting. This appendix covers some techniques that make the production end of output run smoothly.

You can save Photoshop art in any of more than fifteen file formats for exporting to other programs and computer platforms. Only three of the formats—PICT file, EPS, and TIFF—are useful for exporting to and printing from page layout or drawing programs. If you want to exchange files between IBM and Macintosh computers, you can use either TIFF or Photoshop 2.5 format.

PICT FILE

PICT files are useful for previewing high-resolution art accurately in page layout programs and for creating templates used for guides in drawing programs (see Chapter Three, FIGURE 3:3, *Illustrator Templates*). Although you can print a PICT file, the quality is not adequate for final output. If your monitor displays 24 bit color, the PICT file format can be useful for presenting page layouts that contain high-resolution Photoshop files, to clients. After the presentation, the PICT files can be replaced with EPS files for final output. When you save a Photoshop file as a PICT file, you are given resolution choices of 1, 2, 4, 8, 16, or 32 bits/pixel. This determines how many colors can be shown on screen, and is limited by the bit depth of your display (see Chapter One, *Pixels*). Choose 32 bits/pixel if your monitor displays 24 bit color. When you import a 32 bit PICT file into a page layout program, the preview is in 24 bit color, and looks as clear as the original Photoshop file.

EPS

Save files in the EPS format when you are exporting a Photoshop file to create composite film separations that include type and other graphic elements. Bitmap, grayscale, RGB, or CMYK images can all be saved in the EPS format. You can export an RGB image in EPS format, but it is better to convert it to CMYK before exporting it, to take advantage of Photoshop's superior separating capabilities. When you save a CMYK file in the EPS format, you can choose from a number of options that affect the way the file is exported (**FIGURE A:1**). Below is an overview of the options available when you save a CMYK file in EPS format.

PREVIEW: You can determine the way Photoshop art is previewed in the program to which it is exported. If you choose None, no preview appears; 1 bit/pixel sends a black-and-white preview, and 8 bits/pixel sends a 256-color preview. None of

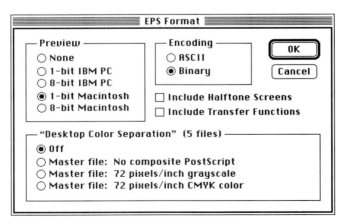

FIGURE A:1

these options affects the print quality of the Photoshop file. However, if the linkage is broken between the Photoshop file and the program to which it is exported, the low-resolution PICT is printed in place of the original file.

ENCODING: Always choose Binary Encoding, unless the program to which you are exporting supports only ASCII. Most programs now support Binary, which creates a file that is about half the size of an ASCII file.

INCLUDE HALFTONE SCREENS AND TRANSFER FUNCTIONS: Both of these options usually should be left unchecked. If you check Include Halftone Screens, the halftone screen frequencies and angles specified in Photoshop's Page Setup dialog box override the halftone frequency specified in the page layout program. This is particularly undesirable when you output color images as film separations. Most high-end imagesetters use proprietary screen angles that should not be changed, since they are designed to eliminate unwanted moiré patterns that can occur in an electronic separation.

If you calibrate your monitor to each output device using the methods described in Chapter Seven, then it is very important *not* to check Include Transfer Functions. Transfer functions are a way of compensating for a miscalibrated imagesetter; for example, if you specify a 35% halftone dot and the imagesetter is printing a 38% halftone dot, you can force the imagesetter to make a 35% dot by specifying a transfer function of 32%, compensating for the 3% gain. A professionally run service bureau or trade shop constantly maintains their equipment so that if you specify a 35% tint with Photoshop, the resulting film output will have a 35% halftone dot. If you check Include Transfer Functions, any transfer functions specified in Page Setup affect the separation, and the calibration adjustments that you have made may no longer be valid.

"DESKTOP COLOR SEPARATION" (5 FILES): Checking the "Desktop Color Separation" (5 files) box saves the CMYK file as five separate files; one file for each of the CMYK separations, plus a fifth master file for placing the art in another program. If you do not check the "Desktop Color Separation" (5 files) box, the CMYK file is saved as one composite file. The advantage of the five-file format is that a low-resolution file is included that is automatically used if you proof the page on a black-and-white or color printer. Choose Master file: 72 pixels/inch grayscale for black-and-white printers, and Master file: 72 pixels/inch CMYK color for proofing on color printers. Pages that include large Photoshop files print out much faster if you include a low-resolution master file.

> *There are some expensive color printers that produce near continuous-tone output (they do not use halftone dots). The Canon Color Copier and the Iris Inkjet printer are the most commonly used printers of this variety. If you print from one of these printers, do not use the five-file format, because you want the high-resolution CMYK file to be printed and not the 72 pixels/inch master file that is included in the five-file format.*

A disadvantage of the five-file format is that it can be difficult to manage the extra files that are created with it. If you are importing numerous CMYK files into a page layout program, save the files as composite CMYK and make your own low-resolution printer files (see Appendix B, *File Management*). Also, ask someone at your service bureau which format they prefer, composite or five-file EPS; depending on the imagesetter, they may have a preference.

TIFF

The TIFF format can be used for printing Photoshop files from another program, but it does not offer as many options as EPS. Most drawing programs accept only EPS files, which usually print faster than TIFF files. Although TIFF files take up slightly less disk space, I prefer EPS for color work.

APPENDIX B
File Management

Long, color documents can be a file-management nightmare. This book is an example of a long document with hundreds of imported color files. This appendix contains the file management system that I used to produce this book.

1. I wrote the text directly in Quark Xpress rather than using a word processing program. This allowed me to assign every element of text a style, as I wrote, from the Style Sheets I had created, and made it easy to manipulate the text when it came time to typeset the book.

2. As I wrote, I quickly created black-and-white, low-resolution, for-placement-only illustrations that the copy editor could reference as the text was edited. I saved the illustrations in EPS format with a 1 bit/pixel preview.

3. When the manuscript was finished, I divided the book into chapters (so that the page layout files were smaller and easier to manage), and flowed the text into the page layout grid. I used the for-placement-only EPS illustrations to make sizing and position decisions. The strategy was to finish as much work as possible before creating the final color illustrations. All of the work up to this point was done with my monitor set at black and white so that I could move through the layout quickly.

4. When the page layout was complete I printed a rough dummy of the book, which included the for-placement-only illustrations (**FIGURE B:1**). On the dummy, I noted the final dimensions of each picture box. Picture box dimensions are shown in Quark's Measurements palette when the box is selected.

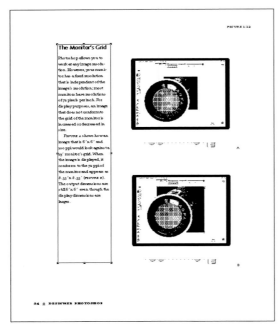

FIGURE B:1

5. When all of the typography and picture placement was complete, I started creating the finished illustrations. Since there are more than 250 figures in the book, I decided to save the EPS files as composite CMYK, rather than in the five-file DCS format. The disadvantage of this strategy was that I could not include the low-resolution master file that comes with the five-file format for proofing efficiently on a laser printer. I wanted to eventually print a dummy on my laser printer that included the finished art, so I created a separate low-resolution file of each figure.

6. Before I started the final illustrations, I created three folders on my hard disk, named Master Art, Low Res Art, and Placed Art. I worked with RGB color in the Photoshop format, and sized each figure to the dimensions that I had noted on the rough dummy. After I finished each color illustration, I saved the RGB file to the Master Art folder. Next I made the conversion to CMYK using the separation table that I had created for the imagesetter that would be used to output the final film separations (see Chapter Seven, *Saving a Separation Table*).

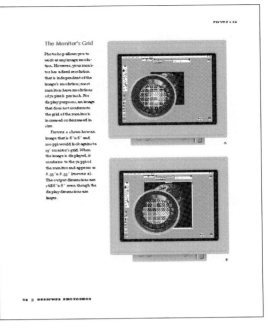

FIGURE B:2

7. After making the conversion, I chose Save As, changed the file format to EPS, and, using the same name (it is very important to keep the same name), saved the file in the Placed Art folder. Finally, I converted the file to grayscale, lowered its resolution to 72 ppi, chose Save As, and saved the file in EPS format to the Low Res Art folder, again keeping the same name. This can be tricky. Be very careful to save each file to the appropriate folder. This may seem like a lengthy process, but the only extra step is making the 72 ppi low-resolution file; under any circumstances, I would need two copies of the color files—one as a backup. The RGB files in the Master Art folder act as the backup.

8. Next, I moved each chapter's page layout into the appropiate Low Res Art folder. I opened each chapter's Quark document, and replaced each of the for-placement-only files with the appropriate low-resolution file. Because I had carefully sized the finished Photoshop art to match the corresponding picture boxes in Quark, it didn't take long to place the finished art. When I had replaced all of the artwork, I could quickly print an accurate finished dummy on my laser printer (**FIGURE B:2**).

Picture Usage			
Name	**Page**	**Type**	**Status**
CHAP 4,5,7:CHAPTER FIVE: LOW RES ART 5:16B	147	EPS	Modified
CHAP 4,5,7:CHAPTER FIVE: LOW RES ART 5:16A	147	EPS	Modified
CHAP 4,5,7:CHAPTER FIVE: LOW RES ART 5:17	148	EPS	Modified
CHAP 4,5,7:CHAPTER FIVE: LOW RES ART 5:18	148	EPS	Modified
CHAP 4,5,7:CHAPTER FIVE: LOW RES ART 5:20	149	EPS	Modified
CHAP 4,5,7:CHAPTER FIVE: LOW RES ART 5:19	149	EPS	Modified
CHAP 4,5,7:CHAPTER FIVE: LOW RES ART 5:21	150	EPS	Modified
CHAP 4,5,7:...: LOW RES ART 5:23 DIALOG	151	EPS	Modified
CHAP 4,5,7:CHAPTER FIVE: LOW RES ART 5:23	151	EPS	Modified

[**Update**]   [**Show Me**]

FIGURE B:3

9. When I was ready to send out for final film, I moved the
   Quark chapters *into* the Placed Art folder, and moved the
   folder to the optical disk, which I would use to transport
   the files. I opened each Quark file and chose Picture Usage
   from Quark's Utilities menu. The Status column showed
   that the pictures had been modified. I selected all of the
   pictures by Shift-clicking on their titles, then clicked Update. This replaced all of the low-resolution files with the
   high-resolution CMYK files (**FIGURE B:3**). After updating
   the pictures in each Quark file, I saved the layouts, and the
   chapters were ready for final output.

 *Even though it is very easy to size, crop, and rotate im-
ported art within a page layout program, the output from
an imagesetter will generally be faster if you size the art in
Photoshop before importing it into the page layout program.*

APPENDIX C
Exporting to Illustrator

Once you have imported a Photoshop file into another program, maintaining the link between the Photoshop file and the page layout is important. Page layout programs usually have picture usage dialog boxes that show the current status of imported art. Adobe Illustrator does not show the status of imported art; separations must be printed from another program—usually Adobe Separator—so maintaining the linkages can be even more difficult. This appendix contains some general guidelines for ensuring that placed art prints properly.

1. I prefer to have the placed Photoshop art in a folder and the Illustrator file outside of the folder, so there is no confusion as to which file should be printed.

2. Save the EPS file's PICT preview as 1 bit/pixel before sending the job out for film separations. If the linkage is somehow broken the PICT preview will print instead of the separations. The 1 bit/pixel PICT will be very obvious to the imagesetter operator and the job can be stopped before it is proofed. If the preview is color (8 bit), the mistake may not be noticed until the job is proofed.

3. Simply moving the files between disks can disturb the linkage between Photoshop and Illustrator. After you move the Illustrator file to the disk that you are sending to your service bureau, either throw away the original files or move them to a new folder (an important step). Next, open the Illustrator file that you have copied to the transport disk; you will be prompted to find any placed Photoshop files. As you are prompted, double-click on the appropriate Photoshop files (make sure you click on the Photoshop files that are in the Placed Art folder, on the transport disk).

The Illustrator file opens and the link with the Photoshop file will be re-established.

If you want your service bureau to open the Illustrator file directly into Adobe Separator, it must be saved with a Preview for either Black&White Macintosh or Color Macintosh. When you click Save, you will be given a choice to save either with or without placed images (unless you have checked Include Placed Images in the Save dialog box, in which case the placed images are saved with the Illustrator file). If you are printing from Adobe Separator, click Save *Without* Placed Images. Click Save with placed images *only* if you plan to move the Illustrator file with placed art into another page layout program. When you include placed images, all of the Photoshop CMYK information is embedded in the Illustrator file; if you include a Photoshop file that is five megabytes the Illustrator file becomes five megabytes also.

APPENDIX D
Faster Photoshop

There are a number of factors beyond the raw speed of your computer that affect Photoshop's performance. Because Photoshop uses its own virtual memory scheme, the way you manage your hard disk and random access memory (RAM) affects the speed of Photoshop operations. This appendix contains some strategies for improving Photoshop's performance.

VIRTUAL MEMORY

Because you may often work on a file that is larger than your computer's available memory, Photoshop employs a method of storing the file and its copies onto your hard disk as you work. This means that as long as you have enough open space on your hard disk, you will never get an out-of-memory warning. Unfortunately, there is a price to pay for this scheme, because reading and writing to the fastest hard disk is about ten times slower than having the file and its copies stored in RAM. You will notice a significant increase in speed if you add memory to your computer.

 Apple's System 7.0 has its own virtual memory scheme, which conflicts with Photoshop's virtual memory scheme. Make sure that you open the system's Memory control panel and turn off Virtual Memory when you are using Photoshop.

MANAGING A HARD DISK

If you work on a file that overflows the available RAM, it is important to properly manage the disk that is used for virtual memory. Below are some ways to manage your hard disk and improve its performance.

- If you have more than one disk attached to your computer, you can choose either one or two of them to be used as virtual memory disks. The disk that you choose is called the *scratch disk*. To designate a scratch disk, choose Scratch Disks from the Preferences submenu under File (choose Virtual Memory if you are using version 2.0). The Scratch Disks dialog box contains a pop-up menu that allows you to choose up to two scratch disks from the disks available on your system.

- If you have multiple disks available, designate the emptiest and fastest disk as the primary scratch disk. A disk's access speed is rated in milliseconds; the disk with the fastest access time should be the scratch disk.

- If possible, use an empty disk as the scratch disk. You must have at least three to five times the size of the file you are working on of combined RAM and empty disk space available, or you will run out of disk space.

- Defragment the scratch disk often if you use it to store files. A defragmenting utility costs $30 to $50, and is used to reorder the files stored on the disk without reformatting the disk. Defragmenting will make all of the empty space on the disk contiguous and will improve the disk's performance when it is used for virtual memory.

MANAGING RAM

If you can avoid using virtual memory, you will notice a profound increase in Photoshop's performance. The rule of three to five times the file size also applies with RAM; if you are working on a 6 MB file, you will need 20 MB to 30 MB of RAM available to Photoshop, or the scratch disk will be used for virtual memory. Below are some tips for managing memory.

- If you purchase more than 8 MB of RAM and your computer is a Macintosh II, IIx, or IIcx, you must be using System 7.0 or later and have an INIT called Mode 32, which Apple distributes free of charge, installed in your System folder. All of your applications and system INITs must be up-to-date (32 bit clean) for this configuration to work.

- If you are using System 6.x, you can access more than 8 MB by creating a RAM disk with a third-party utility (Maxima from Connectix works well). A RAM disk looks and acts like a normal hard disk on your finder, but its access time is much faster. You can designate the RAM disk as the primary scratch disk (the disk used for virtual memory) and your hard disk as the secondary scratch disk, by choosing Scratch Disks from the Preferences menu.

- If you are using System 7.0 on a newer Macintosh (IIci or later) or on an older machine with Mode 32, you must have 32 bit Addressing on in the Memory control panel to access more than 8 MB. Again, all of your software should be the most recent version for this to work.

- If you want to take advantage of extra RAM, you must make it available to Photoshop. While you are in the finder, choose About This Macintosh from the Apple menu, and note the Largest Unused Block Size. Quit Photoshop if it is running, then highlight the Photoshop icon, choose Get Info from the finder's File menu, and change the Current Size to something less than the Largest Unused Block Size. Now, when you launch Photoshop, the amount of RAM that you designated as the Current Size will be accessed. Make a habit of listening to your hard disk work. If you have 32 MB of RAM and you are working on only a 4 MB file and you hear your disk working, you know that you are not accessing the extra RAM.

- Make sure that you use the most economical file size possible that still maintains the quality necessary for the job (see Chapter One, *Comparing Image Resolutions*). Not only are large files slower to work with, they are also more time-consuming to manage.

- Do not make white borders surrounding the art—white pixels take up as much memory as colored pixels.

- If you copy a large section of a high-resolution file, clear it from the clipboard after you paste it by randomly selecting a few pixels and copying them. Any art on the clipboard takes up space in memory.

APPENDIX E
Tips

This Appendix contains some Photoshop tips and tricks that can make your work more efficient.

- Double-clicking on any of the tool icons, with the exception of the Type tool will have some effect:

  RECTANGULAR or ELLIPTICAL MARQUEES: Double-clicking allows you to specify the aspect ratio of a selection, or specify the dimensions of a selection in pixels. Version 2.5 allows you to specify a feather in this dialog box.

  LASSO: Double-clicking allows you to specify a feather for the selection.

  MAGIC WAND: The tolerance or variety of pixels that will be included in the automatic selection can be specified. The tolerance entered in the Magic Wand dialog box also affects the range of pixels added to a selection when Similar or Grow is chosen from the Select menu.

  CROP: You can specify any dimension and/or resolution when you double-click on the Crop tool. This allows you to crop and resize in one operation (see Chapter One, *Accurate Scanning*).

  PEN: When you check Rubber Band, a guide line is included as you lay down a new anchor point.

  GRABBER: If you have altered the size of a window by clicking and dragging on its lower-right corner or zoomed in on the image, double-clicking the Grabber tool allows you to instantly reduce the size of the window so that the entire image can be viewed (FIGURE E:1).

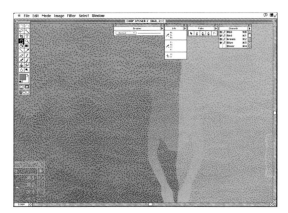
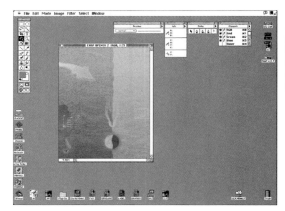

FIGURE E:1

MAGNIFIER: Double-clicking the Magnifier tool instantly reduces or enlarges the window so that the preview's ratio of image pixels to monitor pixels is 1:1 (FIGURE E:2).

PAINT BUCKET: Double-clicking the Paint Bucket tool allows you to adjust its tolerance. Adjusting the tolerance affects which pixels are colored with the foreground color. A higher tolerance number means a wider range of pixels are changed to the foreground color when you use the paint bucket to fill a selection.

BLEND: Double-clicking the Blend tool displays a dialog box that allows you to change the characteristics of a blend.

LINE: Double-clicking the Line tool displays a dialog box that allows you to change the characteristics of a line.

EYEDROPPER: Double-clicking the Eyedropper tool allows you to specify a Sample Size of 1, 3, or 5 pixels square. If you specify 3 x 3 or 5 x 5 Average, the color you choose will be an

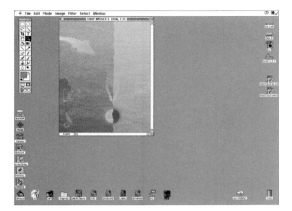

FIGURE E:2

average of the pixels clicked on. This feature is under General Preferences in version 2.0. If you double-click the Eyedropper tool in version 2.0, the Color Picker is set to its defaults.

ERASER: Double-clicking the Eraser tool fills the entire window with the current background color.

PAINTING TOOLS: Double-clicking any painting tool's icon displays a dialog box that allows you to specify a fade-out either to transparent or to the current background color.

SHARPEN AND BLUR TOOL: Option-clicking on the Sharpen and Blur tool's icon, or holding down the Option key while you work with the tool allows you to switch between Sharpen and Blur modes.

DODGE AND BURN TOOL: Option-clicking on the Dodge and Burn tool's icon, or holding down the Option key while you work with the tool, allows you to switch between Dodge and Burn modes.

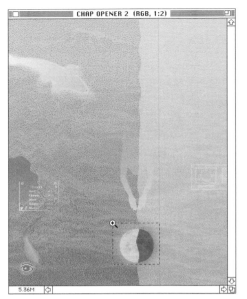
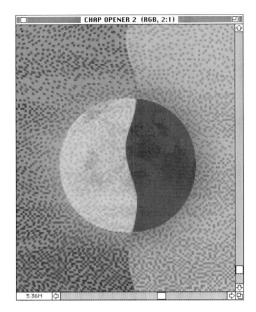

FIGURE E:3

- Clicking and dragging with the Magnifier tool creates a marquee, and when you release the mouse, the area inside of the marquee fills the window (**FIGURE E:3**).

- You can center a floating selection inside a window by cutting (Command+X) and pasting (Command+V).

- Holding down the Option and Command keys before clicking and dragging on a selection moves the selection marquee without moving the selected pixels. Pressing the arrow keys while the Option and Command keys are pressed moves the marquee in one-pixel increments.

- If you have selected multiple areas of an image (**FIGURE E:4**), and you want only one of the areas to remain selected, hold down the Command and Shift keys, and with any of the selection tools, draw a selection marquee around the area that you want to keep selected (**FIGURE E:5**). This deselects the other parts of the image that had been selected (**FIGURE E:6**).

FIGURE E:4

FIGURE E:5

FIGURE E:6

- Some desktop scanners have difficulty scanning shadow areas. To select the shadows and mask the highlight areas of an image, preview the RGB channels separately (Command+1, 2, or 3). Note the channel with the most distinctive shadow areas (usually red). Choose Duplicate from the Calculate submenu under the Image menu. Keep the art you are working on as the Source, choose Red as the Source's Channel, make the Destination New, and click OK. This creates a copy of the red channel. Adjust the contrast of this file until the shadow details fill in (**FIGURE E:7**). Choose Duplicate and specify the adjusted untitled file as the Source, your artwork as the Destination, and Selection as the Destination's channel. Check the Invert box and click OK. This loads the untitled file as a mask with its shadows selected (**FIGURE E:8**). You can now adjust the shadows.

- Masks can be stored as separate documents and then loaded remotely using Duplicate, which can greatly reduce a file's size (see Chapter Four, *Loading Masks Remotely*). If a mask has no gray values, save it as a Pen Path.

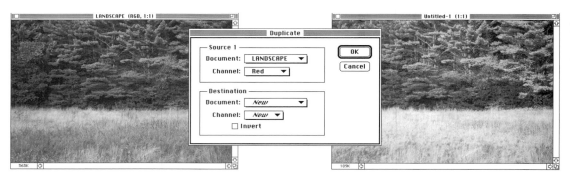

FIGURE E:7

FIGURE E:8

- You can revert specific areas of an image to a version before the last saved version using Duplicate (see Chapter Five, *Reverting Part of an Image*).

- To modify the way a filter is applied to an image, create a new channel and fill it with a percentage of gray that is 50 percent or less, then load the new channel as a selection before applying the filter. A filter will be applied with half as much intensity through a 50 percent gray mask. Choosing Constant from the Calculate menu allows you to create a gray mask instantly: enter a Level from 0 (black) to 255 (white), make the Destination the file you want to modify, and make the Channel New.

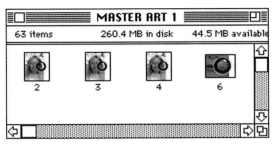

FIGURE E:9

- Check Save Preview Icons in the General Preferences dialog box under the File menu (Command+K) to create a miniature preview that appears in the finder of System 7.0 when View by Icon is chosen from the finder's View menu (**FIGURE E:9**).

- When any of the painting tools are active, typing a number automatically adjusts the selected tool's Opacity in ten-percent increments. Typing 1 adjusts the Opacity to 10%, 2 adjusts Opacity to 20%, and so on.

- If you are working with an 8 bit monitor, temporarily change the image to Index Color for a better preview. Do not, however, *work* in Index Color mode, because it will lower the quality of the output. After previewing the image, return to RGB Color by pressing Command+Z.

- Clicking on the file size indicator in the lower-left corner with the Option key pressed shows information about the file: the number of channels, mode, dimensions in pixels and inches (or however the units are currently set in the Units Preferences under the File menu), and resolution.

- If you are using version 2.0 and do not want to be prompted to Convert Large Clipboard to PICT format each time you quit Photoshop, choose Clipboard from the Preferences submenu under the File menu and choose Disable under Export Resolution.

FIGURE E:10

FIGURE E:11

- If you are scanning black-and-white line art on a 300-ppi
scanner and want to increase the effective resolution of the
scan, scan the art at 300 ppi as a grayscale (**FIGURE E:10**). Increase the scan's resolution to at least 1,000 ppi. Make sure
that Interpolation is set at Bicubic in the Preferences file.
(See Chapter One, *Changing Resolution*). The file size will
become ten times larger and the edges of the line art will be
blurred (**FIGURE E:11**). Choose Levels and move the left and
right Input sliders to the center to sharpen the edges of the
line art (**FIGURE E:12**). Click OK, then choose Bitmap from
the Mode menu. Leave the Input and Output resolution at
1,000 pixels/inch and choose Diffusion Dither as the Conversion Method. The bitmap's file size is an eighth that of the
grayscale, and the line art will print from an imagesetter at
1,000 dpi. Because your monitor can display only 72 ppi, the
art will still appear to have jagged edges, but it will print
smoothly (**FIGURE E:13**).

- If you don't want to constantly zoom in and out of an image
while you are working, create two windows of the same file
by choosing New Window from the Window menu (this does
not create a new file, just a new preview). Leave one window

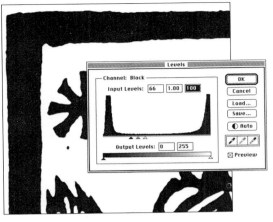

FIGURE E:12

FIGURE E:13

small, so that you can view the entire art. Zoom in on the other window, and when you make changes to the large window, the small window is simultaneously updated.

- One of Photoshop 2.5's new tools is the Dodge and Burn tool. This tool allows you to effectively darken or lighten the values in a specific part of an image. The Dodge and Burn tool is useful only for changing value—it cannot change color. If you are still using version 2.0 or you want to create your own version of the Dodge and Burn tool that is color- or filter-sensitive, try this method:

Choose Duplicate from the Calculate menu; make the Destination and the Destination's Channel New, and click OK. This makes an untitled copy of the file. Adjust the overall value or color of the new file; for instance, you may lighten the values with Levels or apply a filter (**FIGURE E:14**). Next, select the entire duplicate file by choosing All from the Select menu, then choose Define Pattern from the Edit menu. Close the duplicate file without saving it. Double-click on the Rubber Stamp tool and choose Pattern (aligned) from the Option menu (**FIGURE E:15**). Now, any areas of the image that you paint on with the

FIGURE E:14

Rubber Stamp will be adjusted to reflect the changes that you made in the duplicate file (**FIGURE E:16**). By changing the Opacity of the Rubber Stamp, you can make the changes more or less subtle.

 If you are using version 2.5, the above technique can be made easier by using the new Take Snapshot feature. Adjust all of your art or a selected area in some way—change its color or apply a filter, any change will work. Choose Take Snapshot from the Edit menu and then choose Undo. Double-click on the Rubber Stamp tool and choose From Snapshot as the Option. You can now apply the change that you made before undoing to specific areas of your art.

• Setting complex type in Photoshop is very difficult. Try saving a copy of your art as a 72 ppi Illustrator template (see Chapter Three, *Illustrator Templates*) and set the type in Illustrator, using the template as a guide. When you have

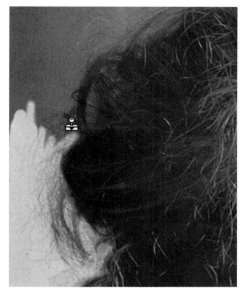

FIGURE E:16

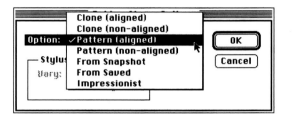

FIGURE E:15

finished setting the type, fill it with white on a black background that has the dimensions of the Photoshop art. Save the Illustrator file with the Preview Option set for Black&White Macintosh. Return to the original Photoshop art, choose New Channel from the mode menu, and then place the Illustrator type in this new channel. You can now load the white type as a mask and fill it with color or imagery.

• When you are making a selection with the Lasso tool, keep the Option key pressed; then, if you accidentally release the mouse button, you will not lose the selection.

• If you are working on a very large file but you need to make extensive changes on only a small section, use the Rectangular selection tool to quickly select the section. Then cut the selection (Command+X), open a new file (Command+N), click OK, and paste the selection (Command+V) into the new file. Save and close the large file and continue to work on the small file. When you have finished making the desired changes, choose All from the Select menu and copy the file (Command+C). Open the large file. With the Magic Wand set at 0 Tolerance and Anti-aliased unchecked, select the white rectangle that was created earlier when you cut the section, and paste the altered selection back in place (Command+V).

- You can quickly adjust where a blend breaks using Levels. Create the blend with a Midpoint Skew of 50%. Choose Levels (Command+L) and move the middle Input slider to adjust the blend's break interactively.

- You can load two masks simultaneously. Choose Add from the Calculate submenu. Under Source 1, choose your art as the Document and one of the masks you want to load as the Channel. Under Source 2, choose your art as the Document and the other mask you want to load as the Channel. Under Destination, choose your art as the Document and Selection as the Channel. Click OK and both masks are loaded.

- You can selectively increase the saturation of an image using any of the painting tools. Choose a foreground color that is completely saturated—any hue will work. Change the Mode in the Brushes palette to Saturation; when you paint, the saturation will increase while the hue and value remain the same. You can also adjust the relative amount of saturation increase by adjusting Opacity in the Brushes palette.

APPENDIX F
Troubleshooting

This Appendix covers some common problems that you may encounter while using Photoshop.

PROBLEM: Painting tools do not work properly.
SOLUTION: The painting tools will not work outside of a selection. Make sure there is not a hidden selection (Command+H). Also, make sure that Darken Only is not the Mode in the Brushes palette if you are painting with a light-valued color on a dark-valued background, or that Lighten Only is not the Mode if you are painting with a dark-valued color on a light-valued background.

PROBLEM: When making color corrections with the color adjustment tools, the changes do not happen interactively.
SOLUTION: Make sure that Use Video LUT Animation is checked in the General Preferences. Also, if your monitor is 24 bit, make sure the monitor is set to Millions of Colors, not Millions of Grays. The Hue/Saturation tool is interactive only in 8 bit mode (256 Colors).

PROBLEM: The masks are missing from a saved file.
SOLUTION: When you save in any format other than Photoshop, masks are deleted from the file. Save the masks as separate documents before converting from Photoshop format to any other format.

PROBLEM: The color of CMYK files seems to change from one work session to the next.
SOLUTION: The Printing Inks Setup and Monitor Setup Preferences affect the CMYK preview, so make sure that you do not arbitrarily change them. These preferences are used to calibrate your display to an output device (see Chapter Seven).

PROBLEM: The color of an image becomes duller when you convert from RGB to CMYK.

SOLUTION: The range of color that is available in CMYK mode is much narrower than in RGB mode. Make sure that you do not select out-of-gamut colors if you plan to have your Photoshop art printed (see Chapter Seven, *RGB and CMYK Color*).

PROBLEM: A pasted object overflows the window into which it is pasted.

SOLUTION: You cannot mix resolutions within a file. If you paste a high resolution selection into a lower resolution window, the pasted selection will appear larger. Try lowering the resolution of the selection before copying and pasting (see Chapter Two, *Cutting and Pasting*).

PROBLEM: Moving a selection leaves behind a silhouette of the selection filled with the background color.

SOLUTION: Once you deselect a floating selection, it is permanently pasted down; if you attempt to reselect and move it, a hole is created in the shape of the selection, filled with the current background color (see Chapter Five, *Reverting Part of an Image*).

PROBLEM: Sampling an image down causes surprisingly poor image quality.

SOLUTION: Make sure Bicubic is the interpolation method set in the General Preferences file. Bicubic resamples an image more accurately than either Bilinear or Nearest Neighbor.

PROBLEM: Photoshop files are not available for placement in Adobe Illustrator.

SOLUTION: Photoshop files must be saved in EPS format before they can be placed in Illustrator. EPS is the only format Illustrator will recognize.

PROBLEM: Photoshop EPS files do not preview or only preview as a black-and-white bitmapped in another program.

SOLUTION: When you save a color Photoshop file in EPS format, you are given three preview options. If you select None there will be no preview, 1 bit/pixel sends a black-and-white bitmapped preview, and 8 bits/pixel sends a color preview to the page layout or drawing program.

PROBLEM: Printing a page layout document with placed-color Photoshop files takes too long to output on a laser printer.

SOLUTION: When you print a document with large placed Photoshop files (more than 1 MB), sending the files to the laser printer can be time-consuming. If the placed files are CMYK, use the "Desktop Color Separation" (5 files) EPS format and include a 72 pixels/inch grayscale master file. Now, when you print the document on a laser printer, a low resolution printer file is sent, instead of the color file. You can also make your own low resolution files for printing and substitute the high resolution color files later (see Appendix B, *File Management*).

PROBLEM: Some Adobe Illustrator strokes or fills are missing, or their color changes radically when they are opened as CMYK color files in Photshop.

SOLUTION: Make sure Overprint is not checked in Illustrator's Paint Style dialog box.

APPENDIX G
Photoshop 2.5

This Appendix lists and describes Photoshop 2.5's new features.

BRUSHES PALETTE: Brushes can be accessed only from the new Brushes palette. You can specify the diameter, hardness, and angle of a brush. You can also make very large brushes, up to 999 pixels wide.

CHANNELS PALETTE: There is a new Channels palette that allows you to manage and view saved masks more effectively.

COMPOSITE CONTROLS: Paste Controls, under the Edit menu, has been renamed Composite Controls.

COLORING MODES: You can now specify Hue, Saturation, Luminosity, Multiply, Screen, and Dissolve as coloring modes in the Brushes palette.

SCREEN REFRESH: Rather than refreshing vertically line-for-line, the windows refresh in a grid pattern from left to right and down. This increases the overall refresh speed.

PREVIEWS FOR ROTATE, SCALE, AND DISTORT: When you use any of the items in the Effects submenu or rotate a selection, you work on a preview rather than on the actual selection. This greatly improves the performance of these tools by letting you quickly view possible variations before making a final decision. It also prevents you from inadvertently lowering the resolution of the selected area, which could happen in 2.0 if you sized a selection down and then up.

INSTANT PREVIEWS: When you make corrections using any of the items in the Adjust submenu under Image, you can choose whether the changes occur interactively to the entire screen or instantly, when you release the mouse button, to just the selected area.

QUICK MASKS: This new feature lets you create masks that are transparent so that you can see the art as you create the mask. Quick Masks make the selection process much easier.

GRAYSCALE CALIBRATION: You can now have the dot gain setting in Printing Inks Setup affect the preview of a grayscale image. This allows you to calibrate for grayscale output.

PATHS PALETTE: The Pen tool has been moved from the tool box to its own floating palette, called the Paths palette. You can now use the Pen tool simultaneously with the other tools.

STROKING PATHS: A stroke can be applied to any path created with the Pen tool using any of the painting tools.

FLOAT COMMAND: Float, under the Select menu, allows you to instantly make a floating copy of any selection.

DODGE AND BURN TOOLS: Allow you to selectively lighten or darken specific areas of an image.

MULTIPLE SCRATCH DISKS: You can now assign two disks as virtual memory disks.

LAB COLOR: LAB is a new color space designed to make printing files from different color printers device-independent.

INFO PALETTE: You can now customize the readout from the Info palette.

TAKE SNAPSHOT: Take Snapshot under the Image menu allows you to make an adjustment to all or part of an image, capture the change, undo the change, and then apply the change to specific areas using the Rubber Stamp tool.

SEPARATION TABLE: It is now easier to save a Separation Table of the Monitor, Printing Inks, and Separation Setup preferences for a specific output device.

VARIATIONS: Variations is a plug-in accessed from the Adjust submenu under Image. It allows you to make color corrections to an image by choosing from various color versions of the original. You can avoid curves and histograms with this new dialog box.

GLOSSARY

ADDITIVE COLOR: Color made by adding light's primary colors (red, green, and blue) together. Additive color is from transmissive sources such as a computer monitor or a photographic slide.

ALPHA CHANNEL: An extra grayscale channel used for saving masks.

ANTI-ALIASED: A method used to make edges in grayscale or color bitmapped images appear smoother by adding pixels of intermediate colors along the edges.

BEZIER CURVE: A method used in object-oriented programs to mathematically define curves using anchor and control points set along the curve.

BICUBIC INTERPOLATION: The most accurate way to add pixels to a bitmapped image when it is resized. The pixels that surround each pixel are considered when adding or subtracting pixels to or from the image.

BIT: The smallest piece of information in binary code; 0's and 1's.

BIT DEPTH: The measure of the number of colors that a monitor is capable of displaying at one time. A 1 bit monitor can display 2 colors (2^2), an 8 bit monitor displays 256 colors (2^8), and a 24 bit monitor can display any of 16.7 million colors (2^{24}).

BLACK GENERATION: A technique used to create the black plate of a CMYK color separation.

BRIGHTNESS: The value of color as it relates to transmissive art (that is, monitors or film transparencies).

BYTE: Eight bits of digital information.

CALIBRATION: The adjustment of a display or output device to match a consistent standard over time.

CMYK COLOR: Cyan, Magenta, Yellow, and Black Color; The primary colors used by the printing press in four-color process printing.

COLOR MODELS: A subset of visible color described with a multidimensional coordinate system; CMYK, RGB, HVS, and HLS are examples of color models.

COLOR SPACE: A three-dimensional coordinate system used to describe different color models. RGB is the most widely used standard.

COLOR TEMPERATURE: The perceived warmth or coolness of white displayed on a monitor, measured in degrees Kelvin.

CONTRACT PROOF: A color proof made from four-color process film used to predict color on press.

CONTRAST: The perceived difference between the light and dark values of an image.

DEVICE INDEPENDENCE: The output of graphic files from different devices so that the results appear the same within the limits of each device.

DITHERED BITMAP: A method for creating the appearance of continuous tone by spacing the same-colored pixels at different intervals.

DPI: Dots Per Inch; the resolution of an output device.

EPS: Encapsulated Postscript File; a file format used to transfer graphic files between programs.

FLOATING SELECTION: A pasted selection before it is deselected and permanently pasted into an image.

GAMMA ADJUSTMENT: The shifting of the middle values of an image along a curve so that the shadows or highlights are compressed.

GAMUT: The total possible range of colors available to an input, display, or output device.

GCR: Gray Component Replacement; replaces the cyan, magenta, or yellow ink used to define an image's shadow areas with black ink, resulting in more control of the color balance on press.

GRAY BALANCE: The combination of cyan, magenta, and yellow ink that produces neutral gray.

GRAYSCALE: An image made up of multiple gray values.

HALFTONE: A device used by printers to create the illusion of continuous tone by printing various- sized dots with one color of ink.

HUE: Pure colors along the spectrum with no black or white added.

IMAGE RESOLUTION: The resolution of a bitmapped image measured in pixels per inch.

IMAGESETTER: A high resolution output device used to output a computer file onto film or resin-coated paper.

INDEX COLOR: A method of displaying color images where the palette of available color is limited to 256 colors or fewer.

K: Kilobyte; 1,024 bytes.

LEVELS: The gray values on a scale of 0 (black) to 255 (white).

LIGHTNESS: The value of color as it is associated with reflective art.

LINE ART: Black and white art with no gray values.

LPI: LINES PER INCH; the resolution of the halftone screen.

MB: Megabyte; 1,024 kilobytes.

MEZZOTINT SCREEN: A traditional graphic arts device that creates the illusion of continuous tone using a random pattern rather than a halftone screen.

NEAREST NEIGHBOR INTERPOLATION: A method for adding pixels to a bitmapped image when it is resized. The color or value of the added pixels is determined by the neighboring pixel (see bicubic interpolation).

NOISE: Pixels added randomly to an image to give it the appearance of graininess.

PICT FILE: A file format used for previewing graphic files in various programs.

PIXEL: Picture Element; the smallest part of a bitmapped image.

POSTERIZE: To reduce a continuous tone image to a limited number of gray or color levels.

PPI: Pixels Per Inch; the resolution of a bitmapped image.

RAM: Random Access Memory; the memory a computer uses to store information as you work. The information in RAM is lost when the computer is turned off.

RAM DISK: Random Access Memory disk; A portion of RAM set aside and made to appear and act as a hard disk in order to improve the computer's performance.

REFLECTIVE ART: Any art that reflects light, such as, photographic prints or paintings.

RESAMPLE: Increasing or decreasing the pixel dimensions of a bitmapped image.

RGB COLOR: Red, Green, and Blue Color; The color displayed on a computer's monitor by adding different quantities of red, green, and blue light to create a wide range of possible color.

SATURATION: The pureness of a color. Adding white or black to a color lowers its saturation.

SCRATCH DISK: The disk used by Photoshop to temporarily store information when there is not enough RAM available.

SEPARATION TABLE: A set of saved preferences used to make conversions from RGB to CMYK color that takes into account differences between output devices.

SUBTRACTIVE COLOR: The color associated with reflective art in which ink absorbs (subtracts) part of the color spectrum and reflects the remaining color.

TOTAL INK LIMIT: The maximum combined density that the four process color inks can have on press and still dry properly.

TIFF: Tagged Image File Format; a file format used to transfer bitmapped images between programs.

TRANSMISSIVE ART: Art that transmits light, such as photographic transparencies or art displayed on a computer's monitor.

TRAP: The area between two complementary colors that overlaps so that if the press goes out of register the paper will not show through.

UCR: Under Color Removal; a method used to save ink costs. Gray, which would be made from a combination of CMY color, is replaced with a percentage of black ink.

UNSHARP MASK: A filter used to accurately sharpen image detail.

VALUE: The lightness or darkness of color independent of hue or saturation.

VIRTUAL MEMORY: A method in which the hard disk is used to temporarily store the file being worked on when not enough RAM is available.

INDEX

DESIGNER PHOTOSHOP

■

was set in Utopia, an Adobe Original typeface family
designed by Robert Slimbach at Adobe Systems. The
captions and sidebar headlines were set in Syntax. The
illustrations were created using Adobe Photoshop
and Adobe Illustrator. The prepress, printing, and
binding was done by R.R. Donnelley & Sons,
Crawfordsville, Indiana.
The book was designed by Virginia Evans.